THE
MENU

*Spiritual Food for
the Hungry Soul*

J. GLOBADIYAH

authorHOUSE®

AuthorHouse™
1663 Liberty Drive
Bloomington, IN 47403
www.authorhouse.com
Phone: 1 (800) 839-8640

King James Version (KJV)
Scriptures were taken from The King James Version of The Bible - Public Domain.

New International Version (NIV)
Holy Bible, New International Version®, NIV® Copyright ©1973, 1978, 1984, 2011 by Biblica, Inc.® Used by permission. All rights reserved worldwide.

Published by AuthorHouse 02/12/2018

ISBN: 978-1-5462-2877-6 (sc)
ISBN: 978-1-5462-2876-9 (e)

Library of Congress Control Number: 2018901939

Print information available on the last page.

Any people depicted in stock imagery provided by Getty Images are models, and such images are being used for illustrative purposes only. Certain stock imagery © Getty Images.

This book is printed on acid-free paper.

Because of the dynamic nature of the Internet, any web addresses or links contained in this book may have changed since publication and may no longer be valid. The views expressed in this work are solely those of the author and do not necessarily reflect the views of the publisher, and the publisher hereby disclaims any responsibility for them.

DEDICATION

Supreme Dedication belongs to
My Beloved Husband and Friend,
"MINISTER JAMES PRINCE GLISSON"
who made his transition
from this life to a better place.
December 1954 – September 2007
"I loved you more than words could ever express"

I took a long ride with this man who was my Husband, my Friend, Confidant, a Father, an Uncle, Cousin and Friend to many. We endured many years together as we learned from one another about this thing called, "Marriage." Indeed, there were bumps and plenty of pot holes that were avoided because our eyes and hearts were fixed on trusting and obeying our Heavenly Father. Jimi (for short), was always on the front line with family and friends. Very understanding, caring and 'oh so comical.' He would always encourage me to take time out of my busy life to write. It took an unforeseen storm to hit that caused the 'light-bulb' of knowledge to shine and inspire me to do so. For such a milestone, I wish that 'my Jimi' was here, in the physical, to rejoice in the victory. It seems, as though, he came into my life but left ever so quickly; leaving behind our two sons, grandchildren, family and friends and an imprint on my heart that will never vanish. One of his favorite Scriptures was 3rd John 1:2, *"Beloved, I wish above all things that thou mayest prosper and be in good health even as thy soul prospereth."* His wish has come to pass and for that I am grateful.

IN MEMORIAM

Of my Parents,
Who have departed physically from me;
But will always be with me in spirit.

My Father, "Otis Hodge"
August 1926 – May 2009

Dad would have enjoyed sitting and listening to my books being read to him. I can only imagine the joy overflowing within Him. He taught me how to love, how to pray and how to stand, in the midst of storms; encouraging me to know that all storms do come to an end. I wish, above all, that I could dance for my Father again… as I so often would as a child. He would sing my favorite song, *"My Lil' Globie Jean,"* and I would dance. He planted something within me that will forever grow and that is a seed of righteousness.

****

My Mother, "Thelma Bracey Hodge"
March 1930 – June 2012

Momma was indeed that victorious woman that Proverbs 31 speaks of. Her lessons, about *life*, was hard; but I learned something from each and every one of them. This book could not have been written without her; for without her, there would not have been *me*. She was a pillar of strength to her children. I am so honored to have had such an awesome woman in my life that was always known to me as my *Mom*.

****

Bettie Glisson, (Mother-in-Law) and James Prince Fleming (Father-in-Law)
I was so very proud to have been their Daughter-
in-Law for over three decades
"See you on the other side!"

SPECIAL ACKNOWLEDGMENTS

"MY SONS"
You are my Anchors!
Decardio Lamont Glisson *and* Derrick Lionell Glisson
You both have been the stabilizing force in my life.
Love and gratitude to each of you!

When it comes down to expressing my love for you guys, you already know that I am a big bucket that runneth over with tears. For you two are the joy of my life, no matter if you're near or far. I don't think I could have made it, if you two weren't my greatest advocates. When I felt like throwing in the towel, you two became my personal Band leaders; cheering me to finish the race. The time that we are spending apart makes our bond unbreakable. I thank the Creator of the Universe for allowing me to bring forth such awesome Sons. My deepest desire, Lamont and Derrick, is for you to forever eat and feed your children from "The Menu." You must always soar high above, while on the mat, of life's difficulties.

To My *Beanies*

(My Awesome Grand-Children)
Dashan
Daquan
Demone'
Derrick, Jr.
JaQuan
Jaheim
Jahanekea
Jimiea

"WITHOUT YOU ALL – THERE WOULD BE NO ME"

TRIBUTE

To My Siblings

Minister Pearl Williams; Patricia Kornegay (deceased); Bettie Wilkins, Junior Hodge (deceased); James Hodge, Viola Magazine; Thelma Hodge and Bishop Marvin Hodge. For all those times, I've written on the walls within our home, on a piece of paper, inside the family Bible or anything that I could have written on; for that, you must have known that someday, I would become a Writer. Thank you for believing in me and loving me. Through the tears, trials, joy and of course, the many laughters. I could not have done this without you! One thing remains between us and that is the love we have for one another. The kind that will never fail and for that, we will continue the legacy of our Parents; carrying the 'unconditional love' torch from 'generation to generation.'

Special Family & Friends

Family, Daughter-in-Laws, Courtney Jackson and Jalinqua Glisson; it is because of you two, that I am one of the proudest Grandmothers, on the Planet! If I never thanked you enough, I thank you now; for your love, patience, endurance and stability in raising my '*Beanies*.' You will forever hold a special place in my heart.

Friends, Ladora Arthur; Elise Green; Cousin Debra York (Thank you for watching over my Grandson Dashan, while he was in school). Ashley Guy; Susie Willis; Minister Cleo Jackson; Pam Haynesworth; Tarnisha Miller; Pastor Joseph Brunson; to ALL of my Nephews, Neices, and Cousins, especially to Tisheik Glisson, Sharay Hodge Ross and Altricia Glisson. Rose Rita Robinson; Arnetta Coleman Dan and Eugenia Holback. Sister-in-Laws, Ruthie and Ella; Brother-in-Laws, John Willliams and Lucious Magazine, whom I will swing dance with at my Book Signing Celebration! Cousin James and Portia Wilson; Beverly Wilson and Geneva Thompson; Igreta Ragin; Minister Cloria Durant; In loving memory, Marie Gibson Jamison. Godmother Ruth Davis; Beverly Osborne; Coretha Brown; Ms. Lucille and Brenda Hastie; and Gloria Wright. Thank you all for your love and support.

My Editor and Publisher, You're the greatest! You made my first book, *The Menu,* so delicious, that it will become a specialty in the lives of readers, who can't live without eating from it, for decades to come.

To all of those who hunger and thirst after righteousness, you shall be filled!

MANY THANKS

Don't dare think for a moment that I was so big and bad to have come up with this brilliant idea to write a book without you. My intention was to continue to enjoy reading other people's books; until I was confronted by many love ones and friends who encouraged me to write. Your encouragement had such an impact on my life that it left me no other choice than to start writing and for that, I give, many thanks, to everyone!

Elder Carolyn Thomas, the heart of a Sister to another Sister, has proven to be glorious. You have such a colorful ray of love, happiness and joy. And with such wit, it causes people to flock to you. Just to hear you speak a kind word or to offer prayer to the broken hearted. When I saw you with such a determination to spiritually bloom in hard soil, I knew that I could continue to run the race that was before me. I am so grateful to have you in my life and to know that we have a shining thread of a forever friendship which was founded on hard soil.

Minster Lynne Davis Massenburg and Pastor Doris Rodwell, Sister, you and your Mother are true Prayer Warriors! When I need prayer, you are always there. It is such an honor to be able to say that the Father has blessed me with true friends who are standing with me through the good times as well as the bad times. Just know Sister Lynne that our meeting was not in vain.

Frenchetta Parker and Shanreka Henderson (Mickey), thank you both for showing up in my life when you did. All the laughter and tears that we shared, I will always remember. Frenchetta, know that I thank you for helping me give birth to the playwright of the *"Funeral Services of Unforgiveness."* We are friends forever!

Tzephanayah Abraham-Ellaka Steve Williams, Nephew, Spiritual teacher and best friend. Through the years, your presence in my life has become invaluable. We conversate about what's going on in our lives, support each other, encourage one another, and most importantly, challenge one another to be the best version of ourselves at all times. You show me so much unconditional love and support. You are always there, not only on the good days, but the not so good ones too. Those days where I thought I couldn't make it through, even! Thank you for keeping the spiritual line of communication open. If I had to write about all that you are to me; it will mean writing another book. Because of you, I can see clearly now; the rain is gone; and you know the rest of the song. Thank you for standing by my side when others couldn't.

Katie Mackey Glisson/aka Mother Mackey (Deceased), and *Loretta Robinson*, I will always be grateful for having such an awesome woman in my life that was known to me as my second Mother-in-Law. She covered me with an umbrella of love and showed me the path to take to become a loving, caring and faithful wife to her Nephew. Thank you and your awesome daughter, *Loretta Robinson*, for helping me raise my sons. You never said, '*No*,' to me…. It was always, '*Yes*,' and for that, I say thank you. You said you were not going to leave this world until you see me and my sons again, but we understand that you had an appointment that no man could keep you from. My remembrance of you will always remain. And to Loretta, you will always hold a special place in my heart, as my Sister! Thank you for holding me down! Thank you for never judging me and most of all thank you for traveling with me and sticking by my side. You showed me that, "*family lives really do matter.*"

Ivia Wilson Smith, (Lil' Ma), Cousin, 'oh my goodness', what an awesome Cousin and Friend you are! A woman of integrity, who never turned away from me during some of our most difficult times. You found strength to grab hold onto until I came to my senses. You always have a word to brighten up my cloudy day; even when yours was dark. I may not be able to cry on your shoulders, but those ears of yours, have heard my many cries. Thank you for being a true friend!

Camilla and George Barnes, After meeting over 30 years ago, I have stood by and watched a friendship blossom into something beautiful. I will always remember what you said about life, "*You must know where you are going and. how you are going to get there.*" You both always encouraged me to hold on. To trust and believe and know that trouble don't last always. Thank you, guys, for all those Sunday visits that kept me from the loneliness of being so far from home and discussing our visions and making them plain while we munched on our '*Twix and Drum Stick Ice Cream.*' There were so many that walked away during the troublesome times in my life, but you were always there, again, encouraging me to hold on. I love you both and I already know that you love me more.

Hilda Harry Fredrick, My dear, It's a great honor to say to you, thank you so much for a wonderful friendship. When we met years ago, you were mourning the passing of your Mother. We became friends in a short period of time. Before the passing of your father, Elder Leverne Harry, he would often say to me, "*Take care of my baby girl*," not knowing that a forever friendship was being birthed. I thank you for taking care of me and making me beautiful outwardly. You will always be the daughter that I never had.

Alfred Glisson/aka My Lil'Brother-in-Law, You were always in the company of your Cousin, Jimi and I; especially when we were dating, years ago!! There were many times we tried but was unsuccessful in getting rid of you. You refused to take '*No*' for an answer, haha! I thank you for those long spiritual conversations that lead us to true principles. Just know that you will forever be my Lil' Brother-in-Law.

Pastors, Bishop Harley Smothers and Asst. Pastor, 1ˢᵗ Lady Stephanie Smothers, When my beloved husband and I were at a spiritual crossroad, wondering which road to take, with such a hunger for the word and truth, we were introduced to you by *Cousin Alfred Glisson*. And a life-long fellowship became inseparable. You guided us onto the right road and imparted true spiritual knowledge. I am so thankful to know such phenomenal Leaders and Teachers, who taught us, as Pupils, well.

Dr. and Pastor Glenette Wilcher, You are indeed a vessel of honor, chosen to do the work of a Servant. I do love and appreciate your coming into my life for such a time that was appointed for us to have met. You reeled me in as a fisherman reels in his catch; little by little making sure it receives the best care and not fall from the line. You then brought out the best in me with Ministering words to a hurting Sister, who is now healed. Thank you so very much!

Elder Larry and Sister Mae Frances Moultrie, It is both proper and fitting for me to say 'thanks' to such awesome friends. Mae, I remember the day that I conversed with you, not thinking that it was going to lead to a lasting friendship between the four of us. I took a journey away from you, in which you never understood. You constantly prayed for your *gutsy friend*, as you labeled me to be. You have taken such great steps with me. All of the calls, beautiful cards, letters and for standing beside me when your friend (my Husband) passed away. Most of all, thank you for having me on board as a friend. *Elder Larry*, I am grateful that along this life's journey, *the Most High*, thought it to be necessary to place you into my family. You have gone the whole nine yards being a friend. There are so many great memories that I will forever cherish within our friendship. It amazes me so just to know that when I needed a friend, the both of you were always there, especially during the time when *Jimi* passed and you were out of town. When Mae called you, there wasn't any hesitation… you cancelled whatever you were doing and came to be with me and my Sons. You, Mae and your children, April, Dana and Pastor Simeon, will forever hold a special place in my life. Thank you, Dana, especially for being a friend and a confidant.

Elizabeth (Liz) Robinson, My Cousin and Best Friend, from the moment we met, I had this deep feeling that we were going to develop a great kin and friendship and it came to pass. You are another Sister added to the rest of my Sisters. You saw what others didn't. You understood what my fight was all about and I thank you for standing with me as a courageous Soldier! Thank you for all those laughs and good times that we have had and will have. Most of all, thank you for all of the support and your unwavering acts of love. I am truly blessed to have you as my Cousin, Friend and Sister.

Francin Houck Dix, Wow, many years have passed and I can still say with all of my heart and soul that you are indeed a best Friend and Confidant. Even before meeting and marrying your Cousin, we were friends. You have stuck right beside me through thick and the thinness of life. You showed me what true friends are made of… that unbreakable bond. The laughter that we shared over the years, have helped me get through some of life's difficult times. From that day that I met you, until now, I can say, you remain the same. Just know that you will forever be my best friend-confidant. Thank you for making the road that I had to travel a lil' easier.

Ms. Tobba Dow/The Program Director, What an awesome Lady you are! You guided me into the direction that I needed to go. Your programs were awesome. I don't care how old you are, you can always learn something and I surely did. Thank you so much for having a tender heart towards all the ladies that came through *MCJ*.

Pastor Timothy McQueen, Last, but of course, certainly not least, you have become such a motivator. You came along at the appointed time and season in my life when a true friend was warranted. Thank you for being big dosages of humor that you gave to me that kept me laughing when at times, I felt like crying. As you always say, "*Sister, laughter is medicine to the soul.*" I do appreciate the the blissfulness of our friendship and most of all, the spiritual conversations. Just know that I'll be at the finish line waiting on your arrival. As our conversations always ended, "*ALL IS WELL AND STAY THE COURSE.*"

Sabrina Thompson, and your two Sons, *Jason and Josh*; *Coretha Brown*; *Ashley, and Alisha*. May you find peace and always have strength to keep it.

Chaplins, Ms. Pittman, Anna Brickley, Trudy Griffin, Ms. Anderson, Ms. Davis and her Sister G. Wilcher and Chaplin Tanya… Thank you ever so much for being such great Spiritual Teachers.

Foreword

As an avid reader, I have come across many styles of writings from various Authors from around the world. One thing in which I personally look for, when reading any work, is how the Author's writing style captivates the reader. To see what he or she sees, to feel the joy, sorrow, sadness, happiness, defeat, victory, and all the emotions that is conveyed within the body of the writing and to experience the quintessential elements that leaves an indelible impression on the minds of the readers. *The Menu, Spiritual Food for the Hungry Soul*, has done such. J. Globadiyah has done a magnificent job in bringing her life's experiences to us in such a way that we share in her times of struggle, tears of anguish, shots of joy, disappointments, setbacks, forgiveness, love, warmth and victories, to speak to the very existence of who we are as humans; traveling through life's journey. If life has dealt you a bad hand, then I encourage you to read, *The Menu*, for it will strengthen your very soul and encourage you along. No matter what circumstances come your way, by reading this book, you can make it through.

-Tzephanyah Abraham-El, aka Steve Williams

About "The Menu"

J. Globadiyah brings to you, a full course meal, served up in her first non-fiction book, *"The Menu,"* subtitled, *"Spiritual Food for the Hungry Soul."* *The Menu* gives a diverse spiritual take on what you can chew and savor as you stay in tune with '*the Word of God.*' And in doing so, you can be both satisfied and fulfilled in your godly walk of life; triumphing over life's challenges.

The Psalmist declares in Psalms 119:103, *"How sweet are your words to my taste; sweeter than a honeycomb to my mouth."* Just know that you don't have to wait in a long line to place your *Order* from *The Menu (The Word)*. It's a buffet, of all you can eat, delectable spiritual food that everyone can afford; because it is free!

At the Table

Chapter 1   He Taught Me To Pray 1

Chapter 2   The Tell It All Neighborhood................................... 4

Chapter 3   An Intimate Relationship.. 7

Chapter 4   Seek-N-Ye Shall Find 10

Chapter 5   His Will Concerning Us 13

Chapter 6   A Shelter In The Time Of Storms 16

Chapter 7   Entertained By An Angel 19

Chapter 8   Unconditional Love 22

Chapter 9   Until Death Do "We" Part 24

Chapter 10 A Friend Called Emily 27

Chapter 11 Dare Not To Give Up 30

Chapter 12 It's My Time 32

Chapter 13 The Assignment Giver.. 35

Chapter 14 Wonderfully Made.. 37

Chapter 15 I Don't Mind Waiting... 39

Chapter 16 The Path Of Life.. 42

Chapter 17 Turn And Take Your Journey................................ 44

Chapter 18 A Time To Mourn 46

Chapter 19 Another Raging Storm... 48

Chapter 20 I'm Listening.. 52

Chapter 21 There's No Place Like Home.................................. 55

Chapter 22 A Little Joy Goes A Long Way 58

Chapter 23 Along Came Forgiveness..61

Chapter 24 From Rags to Righteousness 63

To Go Plates

Chapter 25 A Weeping Widow.. 69

Chapter 26 Speak Life.. 72

Chapter 27 Who Is It?.. 75

Chapter 28 The Blessed Captivity... 78

Chapter 29 Thy Sister's Keeper 80

Chapter 30 You Can Run; But You Can't Hide.............................. 83

Chapter 31 He's Always There... 85

Chapter 32 Blessings In Disguise... 87

Chapter 33 The Strong Will Survive....................................... 90

Chapter 34 A Dove Messenger 92

Chapter 35 No More Chains... 94

Chapter 36 My Praise Is A Weapon....................................... 98

Chapter 37 What's In Your 'Faith' Account? 101

Chapter 38 Again, I Cried... 104

Chapter 39 A Covenant of Protection................................. 106

Chapter 40 Healing Allowed.. 108

Prologue

(Spiritual Food for the Hungry Soul)
FOOD - *THE SOUL*

To my Readers, Loved Ones and Friends:

Please read this section, as Ingredients may cause some allergic reactions. Let me introduce to you a Menu that has a variety of soul changing foods for all of your spiritual wants and needs. It even has a Dictionary/ Concordance throughout the text to help you find your favorite spiritual delight.

"The Menu" contains a strong dosage of spiritual inspirations offered for many who may have experienced trials and triumphs from life's difficulties. I can truly say; that "Eyes have not seen, nor ears heard, neither has it entered into the hearts of men, the things that the Father has prepared (*in The Menu*) for them that love Him", (1st Corinthians 2:9, *Emphasis Mine*).

As you begin to consume items from "The Menu;" your soul will become invigorated by what our Forefathers, who have gone on before us, namely Adam and Eve, when they ate from the tree of the knowledge of good and evil and received the desires of their hearts. Keep in mind, "The Menu" is different from any other 'Menu' that you have ever ordered from. To receive nutrients to sustain you; eat from "The Menu" at all times.

I invite you to dine in these glorious spiritual meals from "The Menu;" prepared by the Chef, our Heavenly Father. And, in the midst of fear, horror and uncertainties, stories of the Father's love, is written in such a way that you will be able to bask in them and stay on the road called Victory! Stories of love in action, gripping testimonies and inspiration will reveal the Author's determination, integrity and challenges that will resonate in your mind, to speak life to your soul.

Within the last eight years, I cannot begin to imagine getting through life without seeking my Heavenly Father's guidance, DAILY! Bringing to Him, all of my deepest and most inner needs and many perplexities. Therefore, I too, eat a balanced meal from "The Menu" (for breakfast, lunch and dinner), with a snack in between; and of course, who could forego one at 'bedtime.' Sometimes, even during the midnight hours, when I become hungry; I turn on the light and grab a quick snack from "The Menu" to nourish myself until daybreak.

A lot of eating one might say, but it's okay because the more you eat; the more spiritual weight you gain. And oftentimes, when you arrive to a Restaurant to dine, you have to wait on a table, but may be given a Menu to browse over, so that when it's time to order; you have a good idea of what you want to eat; therefore, within "The Menu," you can order from the book of Jeremiah, the 8th Chapter, and learn how there is a balm to heal the hurt soul, Isaiah, Chapter 40, you can find strength when you are weak and also back in Jeremiah, 29th Chapter, there is peace (Shalom) while in captivity.

You can sit at any table as there is 'no respect of person' when it comes down to eating from "The Menu." This book will help people of all faiths. So, encourage yourself, open up your ears to hear; your eyes to see and your heart to receive what the Heavenly Father has commanded me to serve unto you from "The Menu," to provide everything you need spiritually to survive your Journey!

Appetizers, *Please*
(APPETIZERS - *THE PRAYERS*)

Before ordering from "*The Menu*," your *Appetizer* (*Prayer*) brings forth the power of prayers that availeth much. As the book of James 5:16 so plainly states, it is a direct contact with the Heavenly Father, "*who is willing and able to meet all of your needs according to His riches and glory.*" Prayers are very effective and will bring forth results.

Our Heavenly Father watches over His word to perform it. That's why '*Appetizers*' are so important because you are making your request known before you partake in your full course meal. Once your '*prayers*' are known, watch Him fulfill His promises. You can have an '*Appetizer*' for whatever you have a need for at *anytime*. David declares in Psalms 55:7, "*Evening, morning and noon, will I pray and cry aloud, and He shall hear my voice.*"

The aspect of the '*Appetizer*' is vital; it is a personal contact with the Father. This will prepare you for ordering from "*The Menu*." Communication and spiritual intimacy with the Father are things we all should long for. They are a part of our relationship with Him. The desire to have an '*Appetizer*,' comes from deep within the heart. It stimulates you to eat from '*The Menu*,' and is the key that unlocks the door.

'*Appetizers*', from "*The Menu*" are the *Prayers of 'Adoration, Thanksgiving, Forgiveness, Healing and Protection.* You see, Phillipians 4:6, says, '*Be careful for nothing, but in everything by 'Prayer,' and supplication with thanksgiving, let your request be made known unto the Father.*"

The awesome power of our prayer requests is knowing that the Father will give us the best answer to meet our need. So, go ahead... I dare you to *taste and see* that the '*Appetizers*' (Prayers) will be heard, EVERYTIME!

The Most Popular
(APPETIZER) PRAYERS

"Adoration"

"Protection"

"Thanksgiving"

"Restoration"

"Forgiveness"

"Deliverance"

"Healing"

"Guidance"

"Blessings"

Super-Sized Appetizers
(RECITAL PRAYERS)

Blessings: Number 6:24-26

Heavenly Father, I pray that you will bless and keep me. And that you will make your face shine upon me and be gracious to me. I pray that you will lift up your countenance upon me and grant me your peace (Shalom).

Protection: Psalms 91:1-4

Heavenly Father, this day I ask you to allow me to dwell in the secret place of the Most High and to abide under the shadow of the Almighty. Thank you for being my Father, my Refuge, my Fortress, in whom I can trust. Continue to cover me with your feathers and let me walk under your wings to take refuge.

Glory: Isaiah 60:1

Heavenly Father, I ask you to let your glory shine upon me. Let others be able to look upon me and see you, in and around me, consistently.

Repentance: Psalms 51:1-4

Have mercy upon me, O' Father. Wash me thoroughly of my iniquity and purify me of my sin. I recognize my transgressions and an ever conscious of my sin. Purge me with hyssop til I am pure, wash me til I am whiter than snow. Hide your face from my sins; and blot out all of my iniquities.

Jabez: 1ˢᵗ Chronicles 4:10

I pray that you will bless me, Heavenly Father, and enlarge my territory. Stand by me and make me suffer 'not' pain from my misfortune.

Hear My Cry: Psalms 61:1-2

Hear my cry, Abba Father, attend unto my prayer. I cry unto you, for my heart is overwhelmed. I pray that you will lead me toe the Rock, that is higher than I.

Waiting: Psalms 62:1-2

O; Father, Creator and King of the Universe; my soul waiteth upon you. From you cometh my salvation. For you are my rock and my salvation; my defense. I shall not be greatly moved.

Distress: Psalms 3:3

Oh, Father, how I do thank and praise you for being my shield; for you are my glory and a lifter up of my head.

To Hear God's Voice: John 10:2-5

Heavenly Father, as it is written, that your sheep know your voice. I am one of your sheep who desire to hear your voice. Teach me to know your voice and to hear you distinctly and clearly. Give me the spirit of discernment to know when you are speaking.

Tasty Sides

(In Old/New Testament Order)

Exodus 1:14	A Big Helping of the Commandments, Law and Statutes
Exodus 34:6	An Abundance of Goodness and Truth
Joshua1:9	A Dish of Strength and Courage
Psalms 23	A Bowl of Soul Restoring
Psalms 30:5	Some Joy that cometh in the Morning; after a Night of Weeping
Psalms 37	A Soother for Anxiety
Psalms 51	Renewed Spirit to Increase the Joy of Salvation
Psalms 91	A Side Order of Angels to Take Charge over thee and Keep Thee
Psalms 119:105	A Lamp to Guide your Feet
Proverbs 3:6	Trusting without using your own devices
Proverbs 4:7	Wisdom Garnished with Understanding
Proverbs 4:27	Need a Path Mark for your Feet?
Proverbs 31:25	Super-Size your Strength & Honor (so in times to come you can rejoice)
Isaiah 26:3	A Scooping of Perfect Peace
Isaiah 40:1	An Order of Renewed Strength
Jeremiah 8	Remedy for Anxiousness
Ezekiel 11:19	Grab a Heart of Flesh to Replace the Stony One
Habakkuk 2:2	20/20 Vision (being made Plain)
Matthew 17:20	Faith the Size of a Mustard Seed

2nd Corinthians 12:9	Some Grace that is Sufficient
Galatians 5:22-23	All the Nutrients you need in your Fruit Bowl
1st Timothy 6:17	Good Faith to Fight
2nd Timothy 1:7	A Healthy heaping of Power, Love and a Sound Mind (to replace your fears)
Hebrews 11:1	A Saturation of Consciousness mixed with Faith
Hebrews 11:1	An Order of 'Now' Faith, 'Not' Later
1st Peter 4:8	Have a helping of Love that Covers a Multitude of Sins
1st Peter 5:7	Casting Care; not for Carry-Out

CHAPTER 1

He Taught Me To Pray

My Daddy was a praying man. He prayed before laying down and rising up. As a child, I couldn't understand why my Daddy and Mama prayed so much. Some of them were long and some were short. Sometimes, he prayed so long, we would fall asleep. And when we went out on Saturday nights, that's when the prayers got longer and longer. He made it a point to pray for each of us, name-by-name. Just think about it; praying for nine children at ten minutes per child… that can be quite lengthy!

After a long Sunday morning Prayer Service (*that's what we called it*), Daddy informed all of us that *we* would have to start participating in Sunday morning prayer *before* breakfast. My thoughts, at this point, are running non-stop. I said to myself, "*What on earth is he talking about?*" We do participate! We get out of bed, get on our knees, close our eyes and bow our heads… so what more does he want us to do and what's the motive? I just knew there had to be one. The thing that was most puzzling to me, was that, as much as Daddy prayed and called out our names; why did we have to participate when we already knew that the Most High was going to answer his prayers before he answered ours. And, on top of that, on Tuesday nights, there was Prayer Service held at our home for anybody who needed prayer, in the entire neighborhood. Seemed as though our home was never without *prayers*.

It would be several weeks before it was my time to pray, therefore, I had time to plan my big escape. Not giving, any thought, mind you, about my siblings. I get it… they were scared too, but it was every man for themselves, in my book. All that was on my mind, was getting out of my turn to pray and making up a good excuse so that Daddy would see through it. I was wishing that something would fall on my lips, swelling them so big that I wouldn't be able to open my mouth. Then I thought, *'well that won't work for if I couldn't say a word; he would have made me moan.'*

The bottom line was that I was just too afraid to *'pray.'* Thinking that I would say the wrong thing; not realizing that there really wasn't a wrong way in praying. Daddy would always tell us, that we had to know who the Father was; but all I can remember was Daddy always praying. *Junior* was admitted to a hospital in Charleston, South Carolina, about a couple of hours away from our home. I often thought, 'why is my brother so far from home, tucked away in a lonely hospital where we couldn't visit him?' Daddy and Mama finally told us that my brother had a brain tumor and needed surgery and how the local hospital wasn't equipped to perform such a tedious surgery to remove it.

After Junior's surgery, months later, my Daddy told us that the Doctor's said that my brother's chance of living was very close to zero. He stood by and watched the Doctor close the curtain, while he said they have done all that they could do; and should my brother live until morning… it would be a miracle. There was a song my Daddy loved to sing, called *"Come On In The Room,"* and now I understand why; because when the Doctors walked out of Junior's room, my Daddy walked in and pulled the curtain open and began to 'pray.' He asked our Heavenly Father to 'come' into his son's room and *'heal'* him.

While Mama's prayers were indeed a companion to my Dad's; he actually made that four hour ride, every day, to be near his son; often leaving Mama behind to take care of the home (and us). And to put the icing on the cake, my Daddy never missed a day from work nor a Sunday from Church. My brother was HEALED and continued to live on. Junior survived his brain tumor for over 53 years! He passed away April 30, 2015.

Over the years, I visualized how Daddy prayed and taught us how to pray, (it was so essential to his life) and that made a tremendous difference in my adult life; knowing how my earthly Father took the time to teach me at an early age the "power of prayer" and there is nothing like having that one-on-one relationship with my Heavenly Father. I believe, as you should too, believe that prayer is not a meaningless ritual that is performed without 'power' but it is to be effective to bring forth results. As I continue to pray, my faith has been increased and my heart rejoices with not only praise but also of thanksgiving.

I am so grateful to have had an earthly Father who taught me how to pray. I often think about what a Minister said about my *'Daddy'* at his Funeral (*Homegoing*) Service. The Minister's daughter had taken very sick at birth and when he prayed; there was no result. Then he reached out to a man that he knew... one who could *'get a prayer through'* and that was my *Daddy, Deacon Hodge*, a mighty *Prayer Warrior*! And yes, the Minister's daughter was healed. *Glory Halleuyah*!

My life has been so enriched just by 'praying.' And I was confident that if the Heavenly Father could answer my Daddy's prayers; mine wouldn't go unanswered. The tapestry of praying will keep a family together!

Thank you, Heavenly Father... for giving me *'great'* Parents. Ones who taught me about the *'power of praying.'* And I know that they are at rest; for their work down here, on earth, was done.

The Tip:
"The effectual fervent prayers of a righteous man availeth much"
James 5:16

CHAPTER 2

* ◆ ◆ ◆ *

The Tell It All Neighborhood

I lived in a neighborhood that consisted of large Families, Teachers, Factory Worker's, Preacher's, Deacon's, Housewives and our *Church*, which was 50 yards away from our front door. As children, living in this neighborhood, we knew that every adult played apart in our lives. They watched out for us; especially if our parents weren't at home. We couldn't even go outside to play without being *squealed on* by a big-mouth neighbor. That's what we used to call the adults.

I can remember hearing a neighbor say to my Mother, *"I saw Globie outside playing hopscotch when you weren't home."* I should have known something was wrong when I found them talking and Mama put her hands on her hips and stomped off of the porch. As she walked passed the weeping willow tree, she broke off what seemed to be a limb, but in all reality, it was only a branch; I knew what was coming next. I must admit, I've always been a daring child. I tried hard to convince myself that I was invisible to the neighbors, but to no avail. It really showed the respect and care each neighbor had one for the other. Times have really changed.

I can't ever remember such a thing as *"break-ins,"* in our neighborhood. I don't think that it was even possible seeing that everybody's eyes were always roaming *to and fro* around their fellow neighbor's property, seeking out anyone that did not belong. Trust me… they knew a stranger if one would have entered. All curtains and doors would stay open wide and the yard gatherings were a place for *all* to see what was happening. I can truly say that there was so much love within our '*tell it all*' neighborhood.

Two teachers, a husband and wife, lived diagonally behind us. One was a Future Farmers of America Teacher and the other was a Future Homemaker Teacher. They were both very likable in the neighborhood; the Wife would actually teach all of *us* young girls how to become respectable. It took me a while to figure it out, that she was also the *'all-seeing-eye'* Teacher, (the one who told on *all* of the children when they misbehaved in school). It seemed like I was always, of course, the one being told on and being children of a *'Deacon'* in the small-knit Church Community, there were *'definitely'* things that we were not allowed *'to do'* or *'to wear.'* But we wanted to be like the *other girls*. One of my Sisters, who lived in New York, at the time, and worked as a Fashion Model, would send me very stylish pants and mini-skirts. I knew I couldn't leave the house wearing such clothes; especially to school, so I would wait until Daddy and Mama left the house for work to slip a pair of those *hot-pants* underneath my skirt, right before the school bus came, and off to school I went.

I could hardly wait to get to school to take off my skirt, and stay out of the Teacher's sight, to switch down the hall. Little did I know that the Teacher had already scoped me out. She stepped boldly over to me, while I was eating lunch with my friends once, leaned over the lunch table to ask, *"Where are your school clothes?"* I answered sarcastically, in part, to show off in front of my friends, *"Can't you see? I have my clothes on!"* But before I could continue, I began to have an anxiety attack about the words that were flowing freely from my mouth and knowing what was going to happen to me when I got home… *'Another branch from the weeping willow tree,'* would be waiting for me right after dinner. So naturally, as soon as I arrived home, I took the telephone receiver off the hook, to keep my Teacher from calling. Lo' and behold, that didn't stop her from coming to the house. *Oh boy*! How I regretted seeing her big station wagon coming into our yard. I wanted so badly to run to her car and tell her, *"If you don't get out of our yard, I will call the Police and have you arrested for trespassing."* Now you already know that was only a thought that never formed into a verbal sentence. I could have only imagined what would have happened if I was able to carry that thought out. It would have cost me my hands, arms, feet, teeth and one remaining dimple. I had had two dimples, but somewhere down the road, one *got* missing.

As I began to think more rationally, the thought came to me… to meet the Teacher at the car before Mama and throw myself at her mercy and whine 'please don't tell on me,' and how I would promise not to wear those type of clothes again. Unfortunately, Mama got to the car before I could. I received a 'whipping' for two things that afternoon. One for taking the telephone receiver off the hook and the second one for wearing those *hot-pants* to school. The *'whipping'* didn't hurt as bad as seeing my hot-pants and mini-skirts being burned up by a fire Mama started in the yard, just for that purpose. Everything went up into a big flame, and of course, the next day, I had to apologize to my Teacher in front of those same friends. Thankfully, she accepted my apology with a long speech; one that energized my soul… Letting me know that I was born to be a *Leader*.

We all have had that *special Teacher* or *Neighbor* who believed in us enough to make us believe in ourselves. So many years later, when I became a Hair-Stylist and an Instructor for the American International Hair Weaving Association, my Parents, Neighbors, Mentor, Auntie Addie Rush, who inspired me to become a Beautician, like herself, and none other than 'my Teacher' was on hand to share in my accomplishment. They were extremely proud to be able to say that another child had rose to greatness from the "*Tell It All Neighborhood.*"

The Tip:
"Thou shalt love thy neighbor as thyself"
Matthew 19:19

CHAPTER 3

✦✦✦✦

An Intimate Relationship

When you think about having an intimate relationship with someone, you think of being in close association, familiar and personal. Think about when you were dating or as the old folks would say, '*Courting*.' You didn't love that person at first. You may have liked him or her, but you just had to get to know them better. I can remember my days of dating. I wasn't sure who wanted to know more about the person; *me or my Parents*. They would even post a special bulletin on who we were dating; especially the girls. They wanted to know everything there was to know about them, such as "*What Neighborhood or City he was from... who his Parents and Grandparents were... what Schools they attended*" and the list goes on and on. And then that final question, "*Why do you want to date my daughter?*" I thought to myself, "WOW!" *What was left for me to find out?*" I called it, "*NSP*," the *Nosey Parent Syndrome*.

I've come to find out that in order to have an intimate relationship with someone, you must first become familiar with that person. The same principle applies to having a relationship with the Heavenly Father. You must first begin by looking into the Word of God (The Menu) to see what is available inside. First, there is an '*Introduction*,' into His Word. This is what He begins to say boldly as He introduces himself, in Genesis 2:24, as the '*Creator of Heaven and Earth*.' And in the book of Exodus, See Chapters 3:13-14 and 20:2, I am Yahweh, thy Elohim, (the LORD our God) who brought you out of the land of Egypt, out of the house of bondage, thou shalt have no other gods before Him and told Moses, respectively, to tell the Children of Israel, who '*He*' was, what *His* name was, and who sent Moses… "*Say to them, the Creator of your Fathers sent me unto you*"… and "*I AM THAT I AM.*" (Paraphrased).

What an introduction! The most powerful introduction in the Universe. Who wouldn't want to know the Person that made such a bold announcement. Such an introduction should cause one's appetite to search for more.

Isaiah, Chapter 43:11, the introduction continues, "*I, even I, am Yahweh and beside me there is no Savior.*" The more you search, the more there is to be revealed and the more revealed, the hungrier you become, *to know* the Person. Keeping in context with the book, (you scan the Menu, for the item you want to partake of… the one that is pleasing to your palate) and looked upon by "*line upon line, precept upon precept, here a little, there a little,*" just like Isaiah 28:11 states.

Now that you've built this intimate relationship, you don't want anyone else; *but your* new boyfriend or girlfriend. Or that would create a little jealousy, right? Guess what? Your Heavenly Father's name is known in Exodus 34:14 as '*Jealous.*' and Exodus 20:5 tells us why He is called, '*Jealous,*' because He does not want us to put other gods or idols before Him. Your '*first*' and your '*last,*' as declared in Isaiah 44:6. (Paraphrased). He is yet making introductions of Himself.

What an awesome resume! I've studied our Heavenly Father's credentials, and found Him to be a loving, trusting Creator of the Universe; whereas nothing is too hard for Him and to know that He loves us; blows my mind. Seeing that you now have the tools to build this intimate relationship with your Heavenly Father, it's time to work on it. He's in love with a 'Sinner' like me, I'd question myself and Him; telling Him what I needed Him to do for me. Isn't that what we do, Ladies?

Here's some of the things that I needed and I know that you have your own wants and wishes; just be sure to write them down, expressing them on paper:

"Create in me, a clean heart and renew a right spirit within me."

"Be a lamp unto my feet and a light unto my path."

"Mold me and shape me."

"Order my steps."

Now that Yahweh has shown His love unto you and I... *What about our love toward Him?* Show your love by spending time in prayer and meditation and by keeping His commandments, laws and statutes. Make Him the *'Lover of your Soul.'* Next, do what we naturally do, run and tell someone about your 'relationship.' Tell of His goodness and mercy. If you are like me, I can't keep it to myself! Has He kept you through a raging storm, like He has done for me? Have you become frustrated by waiting for your meal, when the Chef seemed to be taking too long to prepare it? It takes time, *sometime*, to cook up all the food you ordered and bring it out in a timely manner. Likewise, it takes time to be seasoned. But stay seated, don't leave the table too soon.

The Tip:
"I waited patiently for Yahweh; and He inclined unto me and heard my cry.
He brought me up also out of a horrible pit, out of the miry clay,
and set my feet upon a rock, and established my goings"
Psalms 40:1-2

CHAPTER 4

✦✦✦✦✦

Seek-N-Ye Shall Find

When you seek something, you are in pursuit of it; not stopping until you have found it. No matter how long it takes. That's just like the game we played as children, 'Hide-n-seek." Some of us may still play it with our Children and Grandchildren today. You know how the game is played but just in case, you cannot recall, let me refresh your memory.

The object of the game is to run and hide and have the 'Seeker' try to find you. It is played inside or out. Outside was a little challenging, because, at least in my case, you could run and hide under the house, in the pump house, behind the barn or at a neighbor's house, which most of the time was in the same yard; and if you would have paid close attention to the neighbor's dog, you would have known where to look because the dog would just stand there looking into the direction where you were hiding.

Now inside was much easier; with the house not having many rooms. You were sure to find the 'Hider' under the bed, behind the door, in a closet or in the bathroom. The 'Seeker' was always happy when he or she could find all of the 'hiders' because the reward was the pleasure of getting a spoonful of food off of each 'hiders' plate at dinner time. That meant a lot of food, in my family, because there was so many of us. What a reward that was!

This children's game, although simple and innocent, conveys such meaningful life's principles, that one could use for personal growth. For example, you may have misplaced something that you were desperately in need of; such as money, an important telephone number, eye glasses

10

or maybe that winning lottery ticket; nevertheless, you set out being fully focused trying to find that which was lost because of its value *to you*. That simple children's game teaches one to seek until the very thing you are looking for is found. This is called, '*the principle* of *seeking*.'

I remember my children, especially, my *baby boy*. He loved to frequently hide from me, in any store, when I took him shopping with me. This also posed a serious problem since by *my* having to seek for him, I had to enlist the Store Manager, when I ran out of options. And, at times, this meant locking *all* of the exit doors; searching all of the dressing rooms, bathrooms and then finally finding him under a clothing rack. You already know the reward the '*hider*' received and it wasn't a spoonful of food from his oldest brother's plate either. But of course, I was happy to have found him.

This game is played just for fun but what about seeking and finding Yahweh and receiving that great spiritual reward? That reward is much greater than any lottery ticket or a spoonful of food. "*Seek Yahweh while He may be found, call upon Him while He is near,*" Isaiah 55:6 admonishes and if you look at 2nd Chronicles 15:1, 2, 8 and 12, it says the spirit of Yahweh came upon Azariah, the son of Obed, and he went out to meet Asa and said unto him; "*Hear me, Asa and all of Judah and Benjamin, Yahweh is with you, while you be with Him; and if you seek Him, He will be found of you, but if you forsake Him; He'll forsake you.*" Verse 8, "*and when Asa heard these words and the prophecy of Oded the Prophet, he took courage and put away the abominable idols out of all of the land of Judah and Benjamin and out of the cities which he has taken from mount Ephraim and renewed the altar of Yahweh.*" Verse 12, "*and they entered into a covenant to seek Yahweh, the Creator of their fathers with all their heart and with all their soul.*"

Scripture said that Asa took courage; meaning that he had a 'made up' mind to remove the idols from amongst them. No matter who or what he had to go up against; including his own Mother, who he removed from being Queen because she made an idol and worshipped it. I can imagine that was very hard to do; but it was either the Heavenly Father or his earthly Mother.

Lamentations 3:25, tells us, "*The Father is good to them that wait for Him; to the soul that seeketh Him.*" There's a seriousness in the Scriptures about seeking and finding Yahweh, for sure. Give it all you got! Proverbs 8:7, is plain too, "*If you seek me early, you will find me.*" When I seek after something, my attitude is, '*I am not going to quit until I find it, especially if I really need to find it.*' See also Matthew 7:7, "*Ask, and it shall be given you, 'seek' and ye shall find; knock and it shall be opened unto you.*"

So, start today, get busy seeking Him! Even through life's interruptions, which are many, keep your zeal of 'seeking.' Like my '*Daddy,*' remember? When he sought the Heavenly Father, he found Him to be a healer, a heart fixer and a mind regulator. That didn't make any sense to me back then, but now I fully understand. I sought him too, He was a deliverer, a protector and my rock! And I am here to tell you; that there is none like Him, so continue to seek and you will be sure to find.

The Tip:
"*One thing have I desired of Yahweh, that will I seek after;*
That I may dwell in the house of Yahweh all the days of my life,
To behold the beauty of Yahweh and to enquire in His temple."
Psalms 27:4

CHAPTER 5

❖❖❖❖❖

His Will Concerning Us

O h, how excellent it is to know the Father's *will* concerning us. Just think… He has a personal *will* for, each and every one of us, and no two people are the same. And He knows what is best for you. And life's greatest joy comes from *'finding' out His will* that He has planned for us!

One of the happiest days of my life, was when I got married. I couldn't hardly contain my joy. Everybody knew that we were planning this big wedding, but instead we decided to "elope." That's right; we didn't tell our immediate family; no one knew except my best friend, who just so happened to be my husband's first cousin! Who, ironically, by the way, eloped a year or two earlier; I can't remember. The only sad part was the first man I'd ever love, wouldn't be there… yes… that's right, my Daddy, I robbed him of being able to walk me down the aisle and still feared how he'd handle the news.

Daddy was more disappointed, than hurt, once he found out; because I was dear to his heart. Mama, on the other hand, was more relieved that her and Daddy wouldn't have to spend a whole bunch of money now. She jokingly teased Daddy when she rehearsed, *"Now, Honey, leave those children alone because we did the same thing many years ago, and my Father told you… that one day you were going to have a daughter that would do the same thing to you."* It's amazing how my Grandpa spoke that into existence!

As I look back over the years, I now know that my husband, *Jimi*, was the Heavenly Father's choice for me; just as I was for him. The Father's plan for us always embraces the big things in life; who we marry, our spiritual

13

walk, where we live... work... even when we die (if you don't choose to go before your time, *See Ecclesiastes 7:17*).

Are your seeking the Father's will concerning your life? Ask yourself; how can I discover His plan when faced with difficult decisions and situations? Am I leaning to my own understanding? In light of your personal review of how to fit into His will concerning you; let me give you these guidelines to think about... *"Our Father's thoughts are not our thoughts,"* its left on record, in Isaiah 55:8-9, *"Nor are His ways; as the heavens are higher that the earth, so are my ways higher than your ways."*

In other words, you must entrust your thoughts to Him. It is a matter of praying, and asking the Father to lead and guide you and to make His will known unto you, through wisdom; that you may seek good judgment. Ask Him to show you whether you are resisting His will. If you are, then repent and let Psalms 86:11 become your mantra, *"Teach me your way, O' Father, and I will walk in your truth; give me an undivided heart."*

Unfortunately, we omit the step of committing our decisions, to the Father because we get in such a rush of going into a totally different direction; doing our own thing; while not giving a second thought about asking Him for the right direction. David teaches us about this in 1st Samuel, the 30th Chapter, when he inquired of Yahweh, rather or not to pursue after the troops that burned the City of Ziklag and took the women into captivity. Of course, David was in great distress, but he prayed and encouraged himself in the Father.

Have you ever been faced with a similar situation? If so, how did you deal with it? It is a good thing, you know, to seek righteous advice and guidance. I have had to do this on numerous occasions. The Father has equipped some people with a special gift of wisdom, so when we are faced with difficult decisions, it is helpful to seek their Counsel, and pray they are in tune with the Father.

Proverbs 15:22 even states, *"Plans fail for the lack of counsel but with many advisors they succeed."* Weigh the advice carefully, for the Father, may use people He has ordained to help you understand the situation and discern His will concerning you.

When you seek His will, you can trust that an conviction can prompt you as to which way to go. Read it for yourself, in Isaiah 30"21, "Whether you turn to the right or to the left your ears will hear a voice behind you saying, this is the way; walk in it." The prompting comes from the Holy Spirit guiding us. Halleuyah! This is not a feeling; this is His will. So, don't pull back, once you have been led by the spirit to make a decision. Follow through and remember, you and I are loved by the Father; and He wants us to do *His will*; not ours.

So, on my 25th wedding anniversary, in the year 2000, my Daddy, had the distinct pleasure of walking me down the aisle, as we celebrated this milestone, now if that is not His will concerning me… I don't know what it… Our youth, at that time, and even to this day, are not even living to become 25 years old, but how knew that a quarter of a century, the first man, I have ever loved, was able to get his wish. And I was the happiest woman alive, because God truly gave me a God-fearing, praying man just like my Daddy, to take care of me, just the way it is supposed to be, for you see, *"Eye has not seen, nor ears have heard, neither has it entered into the heart of man, the things that the Father have prepared for them that love Him."* And for that you can certainly stand firm, just as I did, *'til death do you part.'*

The Tip:
"I delight to do thy will O' my Father, thy
Law is within my heart."
Psalms 40:8

CHAPTER 6

◆◆◆◆◆

A Shelter In The Time Of Storms

There are storms that come into our lives, that can really blow hard. And if we are not anchored, in the Most High, they will surely blow us away. When we hear of a storm that is about to occur, we begin to immediately prepare ourselves; especially if it is broadcasted as a severe one. We go further and run out to buy milk, bread, canned goods, water, flash lights, batteries, and the list goes on and on, even for the small ones. While there are some that are always prepared for such storms, and all they need to do, is to *brace themselves*; but then there are some who stay on even after evacuation warnings… to weather the storm. Which one are you?

When physical storms come, you are asked to seek shelter in a safe place; that is, if you can make it to one in time. Ready or not; doing all the right things, hiding in the basement, in the bath tub, or at a shelter; does not necessarily keep you safe. But there is a safe hiding place from life storms, and it is in Yahweh, the Creator of the Universe.

You may have a storm raging in your life such as disappointment, hurt, fear, financial trouble, failed business, marriage, family or even coping with the death of a loved one, just to name a few, and in such cases, all you have to do, is 'slow down,' search for the radar (point of entry), and find out where to drop that anchor! Far beneath the waters, there are mountains of rock and the radar searches to find the right location. Then belts are lowered around the rock, securing the vessel (*which is your soul*), so it can't be moved… until it is time for the anchor *to be moved*.

I remember many years ago, when Hurricane Hugo made its grand appearance, in my hometown of Sumter, South Carolina. It came through with much strength, terrorizing and destroying everything within its path. There were many warnings to seek shelter. My Sister and Brother-in-Law, along with their two children decided to stay and ride the storm out. They were believing that the Most High was going to protect them.

They lived in a single wide trailer, and I thought, that that was a bold decision, being under those living conditions; but who am I? As the storm approached, everything started to happen *and* fast! Electricity went completely out… no telephone connections and nothing left on the outside except for a howling wind; that sounded like a freight train or some big explosion. Nevertheless, my Sister and her family began to seek safety within their home, covering themselves with bed mattresses as they laid on the floor. They could hear the wind underneath their house, popping the trailer ties, one by one, that were anchored in the earth. They began to sing and pray that no harm would come upon them.

All of a sudden, their house began to shake, and it lifted up into the air. By the time their house touched ground again, it was just a ball of tin mingled together (*with them in it*)! There was only silence and darkness that covered them. As my Sister began to cry out for her husband and children, she heard her husband's voice calling back out to her and then she heard the voices of their children, crying for help. She began to crawl under the rummage; feeling her way in the darkness and following their cries until she found them. We were so relieved to learn that their children landed safely back into their arms. Suddenly, there appeared a bright light, from an air mobile patrol. They began to rejoice knowing that help had arrived.

They kept waiting for it to land, *but it never did*. Yet, the only thing my Sister knew, was *the light* was anchored in one position. As the light continued to shine upon them, there came peace, in the midst of the storm, and they all fell asleep.

The dawning of the morning appeared, the light that shineth so brightly, just disappeared right before their eyes and *finally* there came help.

When we are caught, in the midst, of life storms, our Heavenly Father expects us to stand and dominate those storms with faith filled with His words, as recorded in Isaiah 26:3; how '*He will keep him in perfect peace, whose mind is stayed on thee,*' even while you are riding through life's storms.

The Tip:
*"For thou has been a strength to the poor; a strength
to the needy in distress; a refuge from the storm."*
Isaiah 25:4

CHAPTER 7

✦✦✦✦

Entertained By An Angel

Psalm 91 has become one of my favorite passages of Scripture. It is a covering mandate from the Most High... Let me tell you why from this magnificent encounter:

Atlanta, Georgia is known as one of the world's biggest Hair Shows and was a hosting city for this huge vendor. People came from all walks of life to be in attendance during the four-day event; which began on a Friday and ended on a Monday. As I was making preparation for the show, my Sister called and said that some of her friends were also going to attend the event. It was exciting to me, since in their travels, they would have to pass through the City, where I lived and I so wanted them to make a *'pit stop'* to pick me up. My Sister agreed; but my timing wasn't good; as I had to assist my Husband in the Ministry of the Sabbath Service; my weekly custom. (*I stepped out on faith years ago, and against my upbringing, when I began to observe the true day of worship, and embrace the sacred name, to the point of changing my whole business life for the Creator; and prospered in my Cosmetology ventures; so I just couldn't miss Church for the Hair Show*). It was important to me to be fed spiritually before embarking on any journey. But they didn't understand why I refused to miss and didn't want to wait. I was a little sad... because I didn't want to drive alone; so rather than sulk, I made a reservation to fly into Atlanta, later on, that Saturday evening.

The flight was less than an hour, and there the plane landed safely to one of the World's largest airports. It was very crowded; people everywhere! It looked like a freeway; where cars are bumper to bumper. Being all, in an *unknown* place, I began to pray and ask the Father to *'order my steps, in the direction that I must go and that no evil befall me… to remove all fear that was trying to pull me under.'* Faithful, to His promise, the Father supernaturally guided throughout the Airport tunnel, and to the street. I knabbed a taxi cab and went straight to the Hotel. I felt awkward traveling alone, in such a big City. Nevertheless, I pushed my way throughout the busy lobby; finally making it to the Front Desk to check in. I inquired about my Sister and her friends, but they hadn't arrived yet, so I took care of the reservation. Not thinking for one moment that there was evil lurking around; seeking whom it could devour; as I felt an uncomfortable feeling, checking-in, so as I rushed to the nearest 'pay phone,' to call my Sister… to see how far away they were, I looked straightforward. Thankfully, they were just arriving into Atlanta. I gave her the room number, hung up and with a smirky smile, said to myself, *"Huh, so you couldn't wait on me… but I am the first to arrive."* But it was all good, planes are so much faster, and it took the monotony out of a cramped drive.

I made my way through the crowd, to one of the elevators. Standing amongst others, who were waiting to get on the elevator; not realizing all of them were men… I got on and waited for everyone to make it in, as the bell chimed, to close its doors; before selecting the number to the floor that I was registered on. When I made my selection, no one else made theirs. Suddenly, I realized what was happening. I was surrounded by an evil plot. Fear gripped my heart and beads of perspiration popped out on my forehead, causing my makeup to melt away, and my fingertips…cold as ice, from the panic that I had worked up from just *standing* in the midst of danger; having nowhere to turn or hide. At that very moment, Psalm 91 is really singing loudly in my mind. I said, Father, I now realize that I am caught in a web; formed by the enemy. I have nowhere to run but to YOU. Your word declares, "He who dwelleth in the secret place of the Most High, shall abide under the shadow of the Almighty," and you O' Most High "will give your angels charge" concerning me. I need your Angels to bear me up in their hands.

Then there came a voice, out of the band of the evil ones, "Gentlemen, you didn't select a floor." They turned at looked at one another and responded, "Oh… I think we are on the wrong elevator." When the door opened, they got off, along with the man that asked them the question. I went to my room, put my bags down, prayed and called my Sister to alert them of danger in building, and to be on guard. When they arrived, I went back down to the lobby to find the man who kept me from being attacked. Surprisingly, he was nowhere to be found.

When I first started studying Psalm 91, it was kind of hard to comprehend or have faith to believe these promises. But the Most High reminded me that '*faith is not a feeling.*' It is simply choosing to believe what He says and that He is always watching over you and I; even when we are unaware of His presence. He remains everywhere. Omnipresent!

The Tip:
"Be not forgetful to entertain strangers;
For thereby some have entertained Angels unaware."
Hebrews 13:2

CHAPTER 8

◆ ◆ ◆ ◆ ◆

Unconditional Love

My Husband had been in and out of the hospital more than I could count suffering from '*Inoperable Pancreatic Cancer*' and from the debilitating effects of the narcotic pain medications. His body could not tolerate the blows it had been dealt; leaving him very weak along with a tremendous amount of weight loss. Whenever he entered the hospital, we were quite lucid and hopeful of him recovering and returning home. He was always in deep thoughts about death being near and talked about it often. Being a man full of faith, he wasn't afraid of dying but it was having to leave us; he'd say. But one thing for sure, and this I know without a doubt, and that is my Husband's love for his family was "*UNCONDITIONAL*."

One year, to the date of his death, I was reading my Husband's bible, which was usually my custom, since it made me feel closer to him, and there fell out a letter from him to me, and it read:

"My Beautiful Queen, By the time you read this letter, I probably would have laid down and taken my rest from this old world. I am so afraid to leave you; but I've been called and I must answer. But I do want you to know how much I love you and that was from the first moment that I met you during our High School years. I made a vow that you were going to be my Wife, and so you became and you gave me two sons. And for that, I say thank you! Listen Sweetheart, I know that you and my boys are grieving my passing and its okay. Just don't get stuck. You all must continue on. Give my sons and grands a heap of loving because they are going to need it. I am taking my journey through time and space, for I know that I am leaving behind a strong family that will

always remember who they are. Always know that all the strength you need lies within the Word, and know that my spirit lives on."

This type of natural *'Unconditional Love,'* in which I experienced, is not beyond your reach. It is also given to you, spiritually, from the *Most High*. You must just put yourself in the position to receive it. *"My soul thirsts for God, for the living God,"* the Psalmist declares in Psalms 42:1-3, *"When shall I come and appear before God? My tears have been my food day and night."*

It is at moments like these, that you too, can write a letter to the Heavenly Father, let him know how you feel. Are you feeling lonely, afraid, or unloved? He already knows! He is waiting for you to tell him of what's ailing you. The only time I knew my Husband was in pain, was when he would ask, *"Can you drive me to the hospital?"*

Don't wait until the pain is too unbearable to call on the Most High. You don't have to suffer pain and anguish. I would lay down beside my Husband, crying, then he would ask, *"Why are you crying, Sweetheart?"* And when I could not answer, because of the inevitable, my Husband would just hold me close even with the little strength he had. But God wants us to *'cast* our care,' not *carry* our care, *'upon Him for he cares for us!'* (1st Peter 5:7, *paraphrased*).

You see, *'Unconditional love'* will always show up because the Most High *"gives power to the weak, and to those who have no might He increases strength,"* (Isaiah 40:29).

My sons and I were granted an extraordinary gift, from my Husband's and their Father's life. We were loved with a rare intensity! He always said *all he wanted to be was a good Husband, Father and Grandfather* and I would respond, *"You are all that and more."* And, so it is with our Heavenly Father; this *"Unconditional Love,"* is so very synonymous and along with it comes much kindness and forgiveness. *"I have loved you with an everlasting love; therefore with lovingkindness I have drawn you."* (Jeremiah 31:3).

After the passing of my Husband, then the grieving began… And where do we go from here? There's never closure, only a peace, that will continue to satisfy our souls.

The Tip:
"Love endures long and is patient and kind;
Love is never envious; nor boild over with jealousy,
It is not boastful or vainglorious, does not display itself haughtily."
Hebrews 13:2

CHAPTER 9

✦✦✦✦✦

Until Death Do "We" Part

It was a cloudy and rainy evening, as we rode to the Cemetery where my Husband would be laid to rest. It seemed, as though, we were riding for hours. I didn't want to think this was the last ride. Just as my Husband's coffin was being lowered into the ground and the Soldiers gave a salute, the clouds and the rain began to vanish. My sons and I sat in disbelief that the man that we loved was really gone. The Ministers said a few final words, exchange of handshakes and hugs with family and friends, along with tears, was all so surreal. As I was being escorted by my sons back to the Limousine, they both turned and walked back to the grave, watching as their Father's coffin continued to be lowered into the ground. I wanted to break down and cry until my soul was content; but knew that I had to remain strong for them. My Grandchildren were just blown away; knowing that their "Pa-Pa" was gone and wasn't coming back.

In your darkest hours, you will find that in the midst of it all, the Heavenly Father will give you unsurmountable strength, for "*when we are weak, then are we strong,*" (2 Corinthians 12:10, paraphrased). So, no, it was not the time to break! Ecclesiates left on record for us, in Chapter 3:1-4, "*To everything there is a season, a time for every purpose under heaven; a time to be born and a time to die; a time to plant, and, a time to pluck what is planted; a time to kill and a time to heal; a time to break down and a time to build up; a time to weep, and a time to laugh; a time to mourn and a time to dance.*"

So, I went back to the Cemetery alone, the following day. I sat on the ground beside my Husband's grave; just to be near him… wondering where do I go from here; just knowing that my life was never going to be the same. It seemed like the ground around me had a great force; like quick sand that was pulling me deeply into it. Then I remembered, I will not go under, for my life with my Husband was well lived. Tears welled up in my eyes, and for the first time, I allowed them to flow freely. They flowed like a silent river, but the Most High *"numbers our wanderings, putting our tears into His bottle,"* (Psalms 56:8, *paraphrased*).

I felt like my son, when he cried out one day, *"Why did my Partner have to die?"* As we always played *family* games together, and my oldest son would be on my side and my youngest son and his Father were always on the same team. That's how it is with the Heavenly Father, we are on his team, and He had to die for us.

We were married at nineteen and twenty years old, young huh?! We grew together, in love and marriage; waking up daily to a new challenge. Every anniversary was special and unique. One was very funny, in particular, as my Husband was so comical. He told my sons and I to look our best, because it was my birthday and he was taking me out to dinner. We did just that. Dressed up and looking good, bent on finding out what choice of restaurant it would be. Well that restaurant was *"McDonald's!"* Oh how, the boys and I laughed. We could barely order our meal. These are the kind of memories that will forever linger. In the latter part of Nehemiah 8:10, we are admonished, *"Do not sorrow, for the joy of Yahweh is our strength."*

I've fought back many tears, wondering how I was to live without my Husband, my friend, the one I dreamed of living a long life with. The man I deeply loved, bearing his children, having to watch him suffer and knowing that we would not grow old together. He would call me to the kitchen table to show me how to test his blood sugar level. I was always afraid to stick him with the needle. He often said, "It's okay for there will come a time that you probably will have to do this for me." Not knowing the time was so near. This thing called, Pancreatic Cancer, came through like a flood… but isn't that how the enemy tries to come? And you know what happens, *"the Most High lifts up a standard against it!"* Check it out for yourself in Isaiah 59:19.

I often sat and reminisced about being married for over thirty years, and I begin to smile. We vowed to love and cherish one another *"in sickness* and in health," *until death do we part*, so the sting of death came and departed a marriage but not our spirit. *"And God will wipe away every tear from their eyes; there shall be no more death, nor sorrow, nor crying. There shall be no more pain, for the former things have passed away."* (Revelation 21:4). Let this be your comfort as it is mine. You will think about those long nights and days, as you watch or have had to watch a love one endure such a battle, rather it be a physical sickness or mental illness; and while it is not easy being a Care-giver you *can* give care.

The Tip:
"Now she who is really a widow, and left alone,
Trusts in God and continues in supplications
and prayers day and night."
1st Timothy 5:5

CHAPTER 10

A Friend Called Emily

Emily is my friend's name; but most people called her '*Doll Baby.*' The opportunity never presented itself for me to ask the question, "*Why do some people call you Doll Baby?*" I just assumed because she was so pretty. We met when we were in Elementary School. Emily was fun to be around. A lot of the other girls wanted to be her friend, but she chose *me.* How ironic, the Heavenly Father, had the same knack, "*You have not chosen me, but I have chosen you,*" (John 15:16). Some of the teachers, however, didn't want me to be in her company. I didn't know *why* and I really *didn't care.* Isn't that all too common, in our walk with the Heavenly Father, we don't know why He chose us and sometimes we just don't care. Yet, he chooses us for a reason.

It seemed, as though, all the teachers had their eyes on '*Deacon and Mrs. Hodge's' children* (my Parents) *anyway*, just because we went to Church. One Teacher, even called my Daddy, '*Uncle*,' therefore you already know that we couldn't do anything wrong around her. But there was one day, that I intentionally let the school bus leave me, so I could go home with my friend Emily. When my siblings got off of the school bus, and I stayed behind, they didn't know what to do, because Mama and Daddy were still at work. They were scared crazy when my Sister told them that *they didn't know* where I was. I guess that was the worst news a Parent could receive. They began calling a few of my Teachers, and of course, a conversation with one of them led them right to where I was. *Oh boy, did I pay the price for that visit.*

A couple of weeks after all the commotion had died down, Emily stop coming to school. And then there was summer break. After our summer break was over, I was so excited to go back to school, just knowing that my friend was waiting to see me, but she never showed up. Then I began to think what could have happened to our friendship... perhaps she got caught up with re-zoning and sent to another school. I began to pray, asking the Heavenly Father, where my friend could be. It seems like He was taking His time to answer me. I just had to believe without doubting that my prayers were going to be answered.

We tried unsuccessfully to get in *over thirty years of talking within thirty minutes*. Briefly laughing about our *'teen'* days and where we were in life but since we had to go, we agreed to have lunch, *later on*, in the week. I, gleefully, told her that I would call with a time and date. I was so excited to know that I was going to have lunch with my *long lost friend*. Much older and mature now, I began to thank the Heavenly Father, right away, for allowing me to connect once again with my friend. Oftentimes, we lose connection with the Creator of the Universe, and it seems a long haul before we can get back. But the power of prayer is so awesome!

There are times, I notice, that when I pray; I want the Father to answer me right then and there, and when He doesn't, I think that He doesn't hear me. But one thing is for sure, as the old cliché' says, *"He might not come when you want him to; but He is always right on time."* Have you experienced this?

Well the day came when I had to make a call to Emily, she thought it was about what day we would meet up, *again*; but it was to tell her that *my Husband had passed away*; (which just so happened to be that same day that we met at my Cousin's funeral). It was unbelievable that after thirty years of finding my friend, I had come to lose my best friend *of over thirty years*; *my Husband* within the same week. Nevertheless, it was Emily, who called continuously after my Husband's funeral to offer me words of encouragement. She had also experienced deep grief in her life also, but she was able to comfort me. *"Our Heavenly Father,"* she said, *"I know you know him... He will never leave nor forsake you... Just trust Him."* Her warm consolations, made me think of 2nd Corinthians 1:4, *"Who comforts us in all our tribulation; that we may be able to comfort those who are in any trouble, with the comfort, with which we ourselves are comforted by God."*

The Tip:
"A man that have friends must shew himself friendly;
And there is a friend that sticketh closer than a brother."
Proverbs 15:24

Dare Not To Give Up

CHAPTER 11

Dare Not To Give Up

This is a *rare* race that is before us; *to win or to give in.* No matter how bad the conditions of life may be; we must encourage ourselves to keep it moving. *Dare Not To Give Up!* Do not be a *'Quitter!'* Do not have that, *"I can't do it,"* attitude. If I don't know anything else about myself, I know that, I don't give up easily. I got that fighting attitude from my *'Daddy.'*

The book of Galatians 6:9, says *"We shouldn't be weary in well doing, for in due season, we shall reap, if we faint not."* Therefore, you and I must not lose heart nor grow weary, neither faint in acting nobly and doing what is right, for at the appointed time and season, we shall reap the goodness of the Heavenly Father. *'Do you know that the Most High is your strength?'* I do! *"And He makes my feet like hinds feet, and He will allow me to walk upon high places,"* (Psalm 18:33). I've found out that a hind is an animal that can climb a mountain very swiftly. It is known to walk and not stand still in terror. It just continues to walk and make progress, regardless of how things might look or seem.

Reading the fourth Chapter of Proverbs, it says, for us, *'to survey the course that we take and all of our ways will prosper.'* It also says, for us, *'not to swerve to the right or to the left, and to keep our feet from evil'.* I know from experience, that it is so easy to get off course and to give up; but it takes faith to go through. And I also know that the Father has not brought me this far to leave me. How about you? Every day that you awake, that is another day that you have been given strength to endure and *'not to dare give up!'*

There may be some battles that seem endless, but do not think carnally, with a fleshly, worldly mindset. Think spiritually and righteously. Let your mind be transformed, by the instruction of Romans 12:2, *"And do not be conformed to this world, but be transformed by the renewing of your mind; that you may prove what is that good and acceptable and perfect will of God."*

This is a day-to-day process to get rid of all the things that may cause hindrances to your spiritual welfare. The thought comes to mind, can I really leave the past behind and press on toward my destiny? Sometimes, my mind gets to be like a computer that takes in a lot of garbage. In order to clear my mind, I have to go in daily to delete all these stinky thoughts. But to do this, I need some help… so I turn to the best programmer of the mind. For there is none like this programmer. I'm talking about the Creator of the Universe. No matter how bad the conditions of our lives might be; our Heavenly Father knows how to delete and knows how to restore. You may know by now that you probably won't be able to be transformed overnight, but during the process, 'DARE NOT TO GIVE UP!'

The Father will gradually do it; little by little. Take a look in Deuteronomy, the seventh chapter and read where just before the Children of Israel entered into the Promise Land, The Most High told them that He would remove their enemies from before them little by little, lest the beast of the field increase among them. Ego and Pride is that beast that will consume a person if too much is given to them too quickly. The Most High already knows that our flesh can't handle what He has in store for us; all at once. Get rid of our own ego and pride and build up spiritual muscles to help you persevere. Be persistent!

As James, Chapter One, says, *"Happy is the man who keeps on enduring trials, because on becoming approved, He will receive the crown of life, with the Father has promised to those who continue to love Him."*

The Tip:
"Brethren, I count not myself to have apprehended but this one thing I do; forgetting those things which are behind and reaching forth unto those things which are before."
Phillipians 3:13

CHAPTER 12

◆◆◆◆◆

It's My Time

I called my Sister as we both were speeding down two different Interstates to see who would get to the hospital first, to get to our "*Daddy*." We both were lost, so we met up at a gas station. Figures, because we were the two sisters that always traveled but would get lost (*in the places that are familiar to us, at that*)! It's been very few times that we have been able to go directly to our destination. Once we made it, Daddy began smiling. We were so glad to have seen him.

As we began to help make him comfortable, to eat lunch, we started conversating and although he was very weak, he laughed. My Daddy, as I was telling a friend, not so very long ago, was a '*great man.*' One that I was so proud of. A man who was so full of wisdom, knowledge and integrity, who by the way, had *love* for *EVERYBODY*. Once, a friend said to me, "*My dear Sister; while in the presence of your Father, tell him how much you love him… thank him for everything that he has done for you throughout your life. As you are talking, begin to rub his hands, receiving all the wisdom that you can to empower you to continue on life's journey.*" I always kept the matter in mind.

Shortly after visiting our Father, my Sister and I left the hospital, stopped to get something to eat, before our journey back home, but we could not digest the food, as we were so engulfed in tears concerning Daddy; knowing that, within our heart; we felt he would soon be leaving us. Daddy came home a week later, and once again, the both of us, was thrilled, to be able to be with him again. We met up with him, walking slowly, coming across the yard from Church. He made his way into the house, greeted us with a big hug and smile, crying and praising God, in the midst of his tears. And we began to cry also.

Two weeks later, I was back in town, checking on Daddy, along with my Neice. He was sitting on the front porch, looking off into one direction, not hearing or seeing us approaching. As we walked up onto the porch, he began to smile. His breathing was shallow, yet he tried to remain strong. We spoke briefly. I promised him that I had to leave but would return the next day to see him again; so we could have lunch together. He said, '*Okay Globie Jean.*' Not knowing that was going to be my last time sitting on the porch with my Daddy.

Another one of my Sister's called, and that next day, I arrived at the hospital. By the time I arrived, my family members had already gathered around his bedside. It was hard to walk to the area where Daddy was; as it was the same area that my Husband was pronounced dead at. But as I entered the room, he was calling each loved one, '*one-by-one,*' addressing us with parting words that were appropriate. He instructed us very methodically, "*I am about to leave you. I want you to carry on, and know that we all must take this journey.*"

The Nurse and Doctor came into the room, and told us that they were going to airlift Daddy back to the hospital where he had been three weeks earlier. He was so happy about flying. He told the Nurses that he always wanted to fly and that it was '*his time now.*' Oh boy, was he smiling… and the Nurses eyes were filled with water; til they themselves, were trying so hard not to let the floodgates open. We were all outside waving to Daddy, as they prepared for lift-off from the roof of the hospital. This would be his first and final time ever riding in an air-mobile. A few hours later, we arrived at the hospital where Daddy had to be taken to… As we entered Daddy's room, he was so overwhelmed with excitement about his ride. He had asked the Nurses, could he sit by the window even; just to see the beautiful trees and clouds. The Nurses informed him, 'yes,' but they could only lift his head a little bit.

The next day, I returned to the hospital, with my Nephew, (the one whom my Parents raised within our home; my Nephew, brother and friend til this day). Daddy was so happy to see us! I began to rub his hands with some lotion while he remembered the things I used to do as a child.

He talked about how he would sing the song that he made up about me and I would dance along to it. As for my Nephew, he loved going to his basketball games, just to see him and the other players, dunk the ball. The audience got a thrill from Daddy running on the side lines.

Daddy then began to tell us how he was *'tired'* and *'wanted to rest.'* Believe, you me, I never saw anyone who was so ready to die. My siblings and I were adamant about being sure to meet up at precise times to be with our Father, when we last left one another. The next group gathering would be around noon on the upcoming Saturday. But the holy spirit prompted me to leave Church before noon, while me and my daughter-in-law, was right in the midst of our *Sabbath* service. Lo' and behold, when the call came through… we were already traveling to the hospital. It is imperative that whenever you get that urging, or that tug in your heart to do something… don't delay… do it right then and there… You've felt that right?

We were urged to get to the hospital as soon as possible. As soon as I arrived, another Nephew came up to me running, *'something was happening to Daddy,'* he rushed. I went directly to the Nurses Station to inquire about my Daddy, and that's when I noticed that even the Nurses' eyes were red…. *I should have known then*; but I just wasn't comprehending. Sometimes, in the midst of going through an ordeal, you can miss signs everywhere. Nevertheless, I was asked if I wanted to wait for the rest of the family members to arrive before I went in… I said, *'No,'* because I needed to go in just to spend a little extra time with my Daddy before the crowd arrived. Not realizing that *Daddy had just passed.*

My daughter-in-law and I walked in and right away noticed Daddy. He was looking straight at me. I realized that he was very still; the tube in his mouth sent a shock wave through my soul as I remembered seeing my Husband for the last time, in this same state. All I could do, at this point, was to just lay my head on his chest, close my eyes and cry. Then I remembered his favorite words; *"IT'S MY TIME!"*

The Tip:
"I have fought a good fight! I have finished my course!
I have kept the faith!"
2nd Timothy 4:7

CHAPTER 13

* ◆ ◆ ◆ ◆ *

The Assignment Giver

I've gotten through some big bumps and bruises in my life. I am now at the *'Crossroads'* and just as I think I know which road I must take; feeling all confident and ready to press on towards my destiny... here comes a big *'pot hole,'* that interrupted my whole plan of living. That's the problem, you see, most of the time, I was making my own plans. In other words, I was telling my Heavenly Father, how I wanted him to work things out; the things that I had already planned. *Are you guilty of this too?* I didn't find it funny; but I know that the Most High did! He probably said, *"Who does this little gal think she is... telling me how to do my job... Doesn't she know that I am that I am?!"* Believe-you-me; I found Him out!

I didn't want anything more to interrupt my life. The more I tried to get it together, trouble was still coming my way. This *interrupted assignment* had moved me completely out of my comfort zone. Being honest, I did not want to do the *'Assignment.'* I would talk to my Heavenly Father and tell Him, *'This is hard, I don't want to do this! Why me? Out of all the people in the world; you had to interrupt my life.'*

Have you ever thrown a temper-tantrum with the LORD? I was upset, as if that was supposed to make Him change His mind, and take back my Assignment; which was to 'quiet my mind,' so that I could hear His voice.

He will give you everything you need to complete your life's assignment. Read the Bible for yourself, in Joshua 1:9, the Most High told him, *"to be strong and of good courage; and to not be afraid nor be dismayed, that He was going to be with him wheresoever he went."* Now, if He did this for Joshua,

He'll do the same for me. So, I learned that I could not be picky and choosy about what assignment I wanted or else I'd choose only the smallest ones. Ones that no one would know about… ones that I would not have to leave my comfort zones; knowing that as one friend told me, *'our assignments don't come free of challenges.'*

Wouldn't you agree?

Needless to say, all I needed to do, was just listen, to hear His voice. I had to spend time in not only prayer, but meditation and studying His *'Word.'* I had to get to a place in my life, to understand that when adversity comes and seems endless, instead of lamenting and acting crazy, I would rely on the *Word*, for it reminded me that *"if you faint in the day of adversity then your strength is small,"* (Proverbs 24:10).

School Teachers give assignments all the time. And rather it be grade school, high school or college, we work on them diligently; making sure we do not miss the mark, in an effort, to get a passing grade and that grade takes us to another level… so it is with completing our assignments for the Heavenly Father. He will take us to another level, when we pass the grade.

So, I went back to the text book, and continued to read the Book of Joshua. I thought about how Joshua in his own strength could not bring down the Walls of Jericho; only in the mighty strength of our Heavenly Father was he able to rejoice in the victory. All the Most High wanted was for Joshua to trust Him; and likewise, for you and I; we must trust the *'Assignment Giver.'*

The Tip:
"Whenever you deviate to the right or to the left;
Your ears will heed the command from behind you;
Saying, this is the road; follow it."
Isaiah 30:21

CHAPTER 14

✦✦✦✦✦

Wonderfully Made

As a Hairstylist, one of my specialties is '*Hairweaving*,' and if I can't weave it; I'll make you a beautiful wig. This one encounter, I literally, as the saying goes, had to practice what I preached. I had suffered extreme hair loss due to stress, and lo' and behold I had to wear a wig. Going through *Customs*, this one time, in particular, I was asked to remove not only my expensive tinted glasses trimmed with rhinestones, but my '*hair*!' Are you kidding me? 'Not my wig!" I felt like I was being stripped but reality quickly set in; I am fearfully and wonderfully made. I did not come into the world with this stuff. I was really preaching hard to myself, "*Godliness with contentment is great gain, you brought nothing into this world, it is certain, you can take nothing out,*" (1st Timothy 6:6).

Did that help? Not really. We are so spoiled. We are already made, but we tend to try and enhance what the Creator of the Universe has already *so wonderfully made.* I had to dig deep; especially for what came next. One of the Officers, had to take a second look, because now I looked like a totally different person, passing through the line. Do you recognize the '*real you?*' Or do you look in the mirror in total disbelief? I, myself, at times, must take a second look. It helps me when I begin to splash water on my face to behold within that mirror, the real me! The '*Me,*' that I haven't seen for a few years. The '*Grieving Widow-Me*! The '*Me,*' without a wig that was only covering up her beauty, and the tinted glasses that kept me from seeing what my Heavenly Father had wonderfully created, '*Me.*'

So naturally, I move away from the mirror and begin to cry with a heart that was full of joy, knowing that I've just tapped into the beauty of myself, the 'real me,' inwardly and outwardly. That is the whole purpose of a mirror, to reflect, THE REAL YOU! Beauty, flaws and all. So, hold your head up; you are beautiful! Don't be broken by the image.

The Tip:
"I will praise thee; for I am fearfully and
Wonderfully made; marvelous are thy works and
that my soul knoweth right well."
Psalm 139:14

CHAPTER 15

❖❖❖❖❖❖

I Don't Mind Waiting

We live in a world of not wanting to wait. Everything is in the 'NOW' syndrome, not later. Even down to *cooking*. No one wants to wait; so we '*microwave*.' We go shopping on Monday, pay full price for the item; knowing that on Wednesday, it's seventy-five percent off. All because we do not have the patience to wait. Wow!

Isaiah 30:18 says, *"Blessed are those that wait on the Father."* Some of our forefathers, of the Bible, waited patiently on Yahweh. Abraham waited patiently for a promised Son. Jacob waited seven years for a wife and another seven years after being fooled for the wife wanted. The Israelites waited over forty years for their deliverance from bondage. Moses waited four decades for the call to lead and then four more decades for the Promise Land, (for which he did would not enter).

What have you waited patiently for? Or when was the last time you waited patiently for anything from the LORD? Let me ask you further, how do you wait on Him? Or do you want everything 'right now? Psalms 130:6 declares, "My soul waits for the Father more than the Watchman wait for the morning. You have to know by now, that our Heavenly Father, seldom does anything in a hurry; not that He can't, for He can answer us speedily, (Ezra 7:21, Psalms 69:17, Psalms 143:7), but He likes to turn us down on slow and let us simmer for a while; preparing us for a great work. Much like a 'Crock Pot!"

So, let's wait on Him, as we are instructed in Psalms 40:1, *"I waited patiently for Yahweh; and he inclined unto me, and heard my cry."* We must do this with praying and thanksgiving; knowing that He hears the prayers of the righteous, and He will answer us. His ear is attentive to our cry! Father Yahweh, has no respect of person. Just wait on Him with full expectancy; knowing that He is going to show up. Wait with anticipation of His greatness that will be revealed, and with patience of knowing that He will come through for you and I. But, while you are waiting, be assured that He is strengthening you to fight a good fight of faith, one that will bring endurance and perseverance.

Be careful to wait without lodging complaint and outrageous crying, *which I have done,* (in times past), it got me nowhere but to my own *'pity party.'* You do not need a cry of defeat while you are waiting. No… no… no… but rather, we *'through the spirit for the hope of righteousness by faith,'* (Galatians 5:5).

How wonderful it is to know that even Job, in Chapter 14:14, says that *'he will wait until his change comes."* Our change, too, will come… at the appointed time. Our Heavenly Father is not like people who we meet every day, who talk big but have short memories. If He makes a promise, know that it will come to pass. Remind yourself of this daily, as I have had to do. You may feel weak or intimidated during your wait, but keep on waiting. Secondly, you gain a much better perspective while waiting. Get a better view. So, when the waiting period is over, you too, will be able to *mount up on wings like an eagle* and soar. Also, stir up the gift that is within you (store up extra energy, so if your waiting reservoir gets low, you can run and not get tired). Lastly, keep determination while you wait; to grow impatience on the Father, is a fruit of pride. Stay humble!

It's a bad having an attitude about not wanting to wait. That was the mentality of the Israelites that caused them to wander in the Wilderness in the first place, for forty years instead of eleven days. They were not ready to go into the Promise Land to possess it if they couldn't even remain patient and steadfast during a little inconvenience.

In the Book of Hebrews, Chapter 10, tells us without patience and endurance, we will not receive the promise of Yahweh. A great man of God, Friend and Pastor, wrote me once, while I was in my captivity these words, *"The word for today, my dear Sister, is "Wait."* And that's exactly what I did! And I encourage you to do the same thing, so that our Heavenly Father, can manifest His greatness and define your purpose, so go ahead, proclaim it, "*I don't mind waiting!*"

The Tip:
"Wait on Yahweh, be of good courage
and He shall strengthen your heart."
Psalm 37:14

CHAPTER 16

✦✦✦✦✦

The Path Of Life

The challenges of life could be a long uphill path set ablaze with fire that should temper and strengthen one's spirit. I know from first hand experiences, that the path of life holds a lot of things, such as adventure, danger, pleasure, sorrow, pain and other difficulties for which any of these things can take place as life takes on perhaps a surprising direction. Each one has its own challenges and each challenge contains a lesson.

My life's path has been difficult to walk, at times, with so many unforeseen obstacles that may have caused me to 'slow down,' but I did not come to a complete stop. And neither should you; for it will be that much harder to get your engine started again. Choose your path wisely. To keep walking or to stop. Why stop when your steps are already ordered?

Take Isaiah Chapter 40 again into focus, verses 29 through 31, "*Yahweh giveth power to the faint; and to them that have no might, He increaseth strength. But for they that wait upon Him thy strength will be renewed.*" Isn't that good to know? He even "*leadeth us into the path of righteousness for His name sake,*" the Psalmist pronounces in the twenty-third division. So, before you ask the question, '*Is it hard to stay on the right path?*' Let me tell you, '*Yes,*' but can it be done, '*Absolutely!*'

Just remember, as I have to myself, "*In all they ways, acknowledge Him, and He shall direct thy paths,*" (Proverbs 3:6). There are times when I want to take control and handle things myself; you already know that's when egoism creeps in; trying to get you to react before you partake of His word in 'The Menu,' the good Book (the Bible, yes, you know the acronym,

'Basic Instructions Before Leaving Earth, yes that book). It will tell you not to lean to your own understanding, let the Creator *'make straight paths for your feet,'* (Hebrews 12:13).

I have had many doors opened unto me by my Heavenly Father, just by heeding to His voice, and some closed, by not heeding, might I say. But no one is perfect, no not one. This book is written to impel you to walk the path of life that has been already paved and don't deviate from it like I did, because of the love that Yahweh has for me, he got me back on a street called straight, but everyone does not have that testimony. I pray that someone will be healed and converted, and know that I walked enough *wrong* paths to encourage you to stay on the *right* one. Read Matthew 7:14 for yourself, *"Enter ye in at the strait gate; for wide is the gate and broad is the way, that leadeth to destruction and many there be that go thereat."*

The Most High has already made provisions for you and I, by giving His Angels charge over us, to keep us! There are many thorns and thistles as we walk the path of life, and such like things that the world will throw at us to make our path bothered and troublesome, but yet, His Angels are constantly guarding us; like Soldiers, standing guard, *'at attention, alert, watchful, ready to protect,* by any means necessary.

How comforting it is to know that as we travel the paths of life, we do not have to slip up and get off course because *"we have been redeemed... we have been called out by name,"* (Isaiah 43:1-3).

The Tip:
"For He leadeth me in the path of
righteousness for His name sake."
Psalm 23:3

CHAPTER 17

✦ ✦ ✦ ✦ ✦

Turn And Take
Your Journey

We all know that a Wilderness is just what it is; a Wilderness. A place wherein there is a lot of undesirable things that can bring harm to you. The Children of Israel wanted to turn back many times to the land of Egypt, but they gave deep thoughts to returning to a place with no future or hope. Yahweh had a plan for His children and it wasn't to harm them, but it was to give them a future. Yet they had to 'turn and take their journey' through the Wilderness, to get to that future; which was the Promise Land flowing with milk and honey.

In Deuteronomy, Chapter One, is where Moses spoke to the Children of Israel. Verses 5-7 says, *"On this side of Jordan, in the land of Moab, declaring this law."* He said, *"Our Father spoke to us in Horeb, saying, "Ye have dwelt long enough in this mountain, turn and take your journey."* When I think about Moses leading the Israelites out of Egpyt, out of their bondage, how an eleven days wilderness journey turned into forty years. *Why?* Because of their disobedience. Yes, with my right hand raised up, that's me! Some things as the previous chapter, *'the Path of Life,'* dealt with; reminds me that it was things during my journey that I could have spent *days* getting control of; but those same things lasted for *years. Why?* Because of my own disobedience. Can you relate?

Now the Father didn't promise them that the journey *through* the Wilderness was going to be easy, but He did promise to be *with them* and

44

not to forsake them, but of course they had to do something in return and that was to be obedient; (to trust and obey). Oftentimes, we deter our very own selves, when we do the opposite of what was commanded of us. Moses said in the same book of Deuteronomy, Chapter 5, that *"the Most High made a covenant with us in Horeb. The Most High didn't make that covenant with our Fathers, but He made it with us, who are alive today. Saying, oh, that there were such a heart in them, that they would fear me and keep all of my commandments always; that it might be well with them and their children forever."*

Just think how Yahweh kept the Israelites wandering in the Wilderness for forty years; whereas their clothes didn't wax old and they didn't go hungry. All without supermarkets nor Walmart stores!

And further, before the Israelites exited bondage, In Exodus 12:1-4, the Most High said unto Abram; *"Get thee out of thy Country, from around thy kin folks, and from thy Father's house, unto a land that I will show thee. I will make of thee a great Nation and will bless thee and make thy name great,"* and then He turned around and told him, *"And thou shall be a blessing."* The Most High told Abram, *"I am going to bless them that blesseth you and curse them that curseth you, and all the families of the earth shall be blessed."* Not one or two families, but ALL the families shall be blessed. So, Abram trusted and obeyed the Most High and turned and took his journey!

When you are taking your journey, just know that the Father is with you and He will make your enemy bless you and those that curseth you, He will curse them and make them to be at peace (Shalom) with you.

Take a look at Job, Chapter five and verse twelve, where it tells you how the Most High will disappoint the devices of the evil one so that their hands cannot perform their plan. Trust the Father through it all as you *'turn and take your journey!'*

The Tip:
"Trust in the Father, and do good, so shalt thou dwell in the land
And verily thou shalt be fed. Delight thyself also in Him, and He shall
Give thee the desires of thine heart. Commit thy ways unto the Father;
Trust Him and He shall bring it to pass."
Psalms 37:3-5

CHAPTER 18

✦ ✦ ✦ ✦

A Time To Mourn

There was a season of losses in my life that were very difficult for me to deal with. Namely, losing my *beloved husband of thirty-seven years*, and my *forever, 'Daddy.'* Even when I received the news about my Mother's death; struck me like a bolt of lightning. I fell and pressed my face to the cold floor, hoping that I could have dug a hole to bury myself. I could have made a river with the many tears I cried.

Being that I was in a different County *and* State altogether prevented me from being able to attend the funerals of some of my loved ones, and I *was unable* to mourn *but so much* or else I would have had to be admitted into a special Hospital (*within a Mental Ward unit* no less), so my initial outpour '*time*' was it; particularly, if I didn't want to be deemed as '*crazy*,' and you know what's next, '*drugs and a straight jacket.*' Fearful of that? "*YES!*" Because some of the feelings that come along with grief are *blame, guilt, hopelessness, and heartache*. I had to stay hopeful that there would be a '*time to mourn.*"

SIDEBAR: If you are vulnerable and hurting, 'your mind can go' *regardless* of how many scriptures you know. *Selah*! (Pause and think about that).

Learning of another death, month after month, nightmares terrorized my soul and it took all that was within me '*not to break.*' My '*fear to mourn*' served as a common denominator to my '*fear to be set free.*' Oh, how I longed to be free, but each day, I mourned less. And with the help of my *kind* Nephew, I was able to survive, my '*Assignment.*' Have you been taking this journey with me? Remember the '*Assignment Giver.*' Don't forget... it's not what you go through, its knowing who's *carrying you through* that will cause you to see the light at the end of the tunnel. Well, my Nephew, through the guidance of the spirit, was able to tap into my heart when he offered these words: *"Auntie, it is not inappropriate to mourn,"* that became my saving grace. He admonished me to *'remember who is with me through all of my trials and tribulations.* He continued to tell me that *if I had any doubt, that all I needed to do, was to look back and see who has kept me thus far and that I did not have to be afraid to face my fears, that they were only an illusion…. Pour your soul out to create power*!

The Most High allows us time to mourn for our loved ones who have passed away. *This gives us time to cleanse our soul and spirit from burdens*, (Read, Genesis 50:1-4, Numbers 20:29, 1st Chronicles 7:22, Deuteronomy 34th Chapter, 2nd Samuel 1:12). *Thanks, Nephew*!

I now, even like the most popular acronyms, for 'FEAR'… *False Evidence Appearing Real*. That is part of my story on my journey through the *path of life* as I *take my turn*. And through much prayers and meditation, I was delivered out of the lion's den, *literally* and I've come to know, however, that *FEAR IS VERY MUCH REAL* and must be channeled properly, til 'FEAR' becomes *'Flee Everything and Run.'*

I was giving it power to control me and it wasn't until I began to approach it as *David*, when he declared in Psalms 23:4, *"Yea, though I walk through the valley of the shadow of death (of the deepest darkness), I fear no evil (no harm), for you are with me. Your rod, and your staff they comfort me,"* that I received a breakthrough.

I now realize that death is not the end of life, and *it's not the end of my life* and I didn't die; though I very well could have. But the Most High kept my heart and my mind. I know that through my ordeal, the Most High delivered me from *'dangers seen and unseen,'* and although my life will never be the same, I embrace fear because it involves change and change involves loss, and the losses changed me. Changed me, to the point, where I was able to relinquish the grip of fear. My relatives are resting safe in the arms of my Heavenly Father. For that reason, I rejoice! How about you, have you abandoned your fears? Are you, too, free to mourn?

The Tip:
"A season is set for everything… there's a time for
every experience under Heaven… A time to mourn and a time to dance."
Ecclesiastes 3:1 and 4

CHAPTER 19

+ ◆ ◆ ◆ ◆ +

Another Raging Storm

As I stood at the window within the dining hall, at the Camp, just enjoying looking the view of the beautiful blue sky, I became captivated by puffs of white clouds, that were just breathtaking. I contemplated on what time to call my family to celebrate with them; this being the sixth year of the family Patriarch's death, our *'Daddy.'* As noon approached, I was really feeling like I did on that very day; the day that I walked into Daddy's room, at the hospital. *Breathless.* Seeing him lying there *lifeless.*

I began to talk to a companion, who sat next to me. I told her that I had had a dream about my Father, earlier that week, and how I felt like something was going to happen. *I just didn't know what!* I told her the only thing that I knew *to do* was "PRAY," and to trust the *Father* for guidance. As we continued to talk and laugh about all sorts of little funny things, there came a urgent call over the intercom system. A sound system that literally reaches throughout the entire Camp; for me to report to the *'Camp Message Center.'* Quite naturally, you never want this type of beckoning. Laughter between us ceased. My stomach turned into knots. *Why me?* It was too close to the 4:00 pm *'National Count to Clear,'* and I just couldn't understand why they were calling me.

'Why call me Lord, Lord, and do not the things I say?' I hear you loud and clear, *Luke 6:46.* Could someone have blamed me for something? Now, I even became *'Doubting Thomas,'* but there was just no way I could be in trouble... I had had enough of trouble which landed me in this Camp,

in the first place; so, I surely didn't want any trouble. *Humpf!* Just let me finish my assignment and I'm out of here.

Right then and there, an Officer came out of the kitchen, as I was approaching the side door, to reach the Message Center…. My heart was beating at least 10x its normal rate. I though he came to unlock the door for me; which he did, but also walked out directly behind me. That was odd… now he's following me. I took a short cut, picking up pace, and we still arrived at the Center at the same time. At this point, so many thoughts are running through my mind. The most important one was, 'Am I in trouble?' and if so, the '*Shu*' awaited me. The '*Shu*,' was short for '*Special Housing Unit*,' located AT THE COUNTY JAIL! I wasn't so much fearful of going to the '*County Jail*,'…. I just wanted to know "for what?!" You just couldn't take anything for granted, since other inmates would do a '*cop-out*,' or also known as a '*plea-deal*' against someone else (*even if it was a lie*; which majority of the time it was), *just to get released*… so to the '*County Jail*,' you'd go until the investigation was completed. Again, thoughts racing, '*Surely, not me! I get along with everybody; keep my distance, and stay in my lane, AWAY from trouble*.'

I was greeted by this tall guy, as I approached the door, who interrogated me, (Name, number, date of birth, etc. etc.). After, I confirmed my identity and showed the various epithtets, I was asked to have a seat. All I am thinking at this point, is "*What have I done*," and "*Oh, Father, I really need your help*." The man introduced himself, *finally* and stated to me that my *Sister* called… my '*Brother*,' passed away. I charged out of the *Center*, running, crying and looking up at the sky. That same, once beautifully adorned *puffs of clear white clouds* had turned into dreadful darkness, just as I stumbled into one of my companions, who had to run me down, as she chased so fast towards me; to console my aching heart.

It was so hard to digest this news; this was the same day, *Daddy* had passed. I became despondent with great sorrow. It became clear to me that I was thrust into another raging storm. It seemed as another loved one passed away, the storms grew bigger and bigger; especially when I would be unable to attend another *immediate* family member's funeral.

After being calmed for a few moments, I was escorted to the *Chaplin*, to return the phone call to the one who called with the news. Lo' and behold, it was one of my best friends; and the same person who had to, by request of the family, to get in contact with the Chaplin concerning my Mother's death. A friend who has stuck with me through 'thick and thin!' *Yes, a 'Sister,' indeed*! Through the *good times and the bad times*… it hurt her just as much to have to deliver the news; and the Officers looked just as distraught as we conversated. We basically cried on the phone instead of speaking. One of the two of my companions, "*Sisters*," also, if you will, was instructed to walk me back to the Unit. The team of support was waiting to greet me as we returned to the Unit, to be sure I was alright; but by my tears, they could sense that something was terribly wrong. I laid across the bed, surrounded by praying and caring women.

When the storms keep raging in our lives, we can always call on our Heavenly Father for refuge and strength. He is the only one, Mark 4:39 reminds us, that can calm the vicious waves, '*Peace! Be Still*,' then the wind died down and it was completely calm. He will rebuke the winds and speak to the waves in our lives…. Just stay anchored, as the popular song bellows, *And ride it out*…

A few days later, I was told to speak to the Chaplin, something had to be done. If you sit back and do nothing; then nothing would happen… So, I had to do "SOMETHING." I prayed that the Heavenly Father direct me in the path to go, and my Parents would always tell us, "Where there's a will… there's a way." Why can't I go to my loved one funeral? I asked repeatedly asked for a furlough, to be with my family, to no avail, do I dare to give up now? I realized that it was happening all around me, however.

Late in the midnight hours, I laid awake; asking the Father to show forth His grace and mercy towards me. I had seen so many things that He had done in my life that taught me how to trust Him even the more… to trust Him for all I had not seen and then I fell into a peaceful sleep. When Monday morning came, I was up early, writing down everything that I needed to do and a list of everybody I needed to see. My Brother's funeral, would be *Thursday*, so I had 'work' to do. A few of the other ladies had 'Escorts,' so I would need that too, and I would need money in my account 'to go,' (who knew?). Nevertheless, by the end of the day some things were in place! Yet, I still had roadblocks… After speaking with the staff member, who was supposed to facilitate the furlough, gave up hope; indicating that the terms didn't look promising since Tuesday and Wednesday, he was going to be out of the office and would be unable to have all of the necessary paperwork completed in time. I wanted to say, "LOOK ALL I HAVE IS TODAY," but I couldn't be too hasty. The tongue is an unruly member and can not be tamed, at least that's what the Book of James lets me know, and guess what I believe it! (James 3:5-7). Everything was quiet on Tuesday and so was I… By Wednesday, I was given approval that I could call my family members and share the good news… I was being furloughed! And I would be entrusted into the hands of my best friend to pick me up and drive me home!

Exodus 14:14 lets us know, all we have to do is "*hold our peace, and Yahweh will fight for us,*" (*emphasis mine*). I had an opportunity through another raging storm to talk to my sons, my siblings, best friends and so many countless other family members… and while I would have to return soon… I knew, *more than ever,* that '*this too shall pass.*' But for now, I could fill a bucket of water with all the '*happy*' tears I cried as we approached the *South Carolina State Line* so that I could spend time with my family. *Thanks to my Heavenly Father, The Chef!*

The Tip:
"Weeping may endure for a night but
Joy cometh in the morning."
Psalms 30:5

CHAPTER 20

✦ ✦ ✦

I'm Listening

A Mother knows her baby *"Cries,"* she knows when there's a cry of hunger; a cry of pain, or a cry for attention. She stands still, in the moment, to decipher the cry. She may even be in another room… but she knows the cry and she becomes a '*Rescuer.*'

The Book of 1ˢᵗ Samuel, Chapter 1 tells the story of Hannah. The Most High closed up Hannah's womb, whereas she could not have children. She was indeed teased by her Husband's other wife, who had had two sons already. But Hannah was a praying woman and she was in constant prayer about wanting a child. She cried and prayed so much, the Priest thought she was drunk. Hannah even made a vow to Yahweh saying: *"O' Father, if thou will indeed look on my affliction, and remember me and not forget me and give me a man child, I'll give him unto you all the days of his life."*

Hannah responded to the Priest, when he saw only her lips moving but did not hear her voice that she was a woman of a sorrowful spirit and had not been drinking as he supposed; and that she was only pouring out her soul to Yahweh; so the Priest bidded her to go in 'peace.' And may Yahweh grant unto her the petition she asked of Him. As time passed, you'll find as you re-read it for yourself, that Hannah conceived and had a son and called him, *Samuel,* meaning '*I have asked for him from Yahweh,*' (verse 20). She did just as she vowed and gave Samuel back to Him. After Samuel's weaning was completed, she took him to Temple and gave him unto Eli, the Priest. She rejoiced unto Yahweh, saying: *"There's none as holy as you are Father, there's none beside you; neither is there any Rock like you!"*

HALLEUYAH. Samuel was yet a child that continued to grow, as a man, in the *favor* of Yahweh, and he ministered unto the Father before Eli.

Chapter 3 goes further to tell us that Samuel did not yet know Yahweh, neither was the word of Yahweh revealed unto him, but Yahweh began to call out to Samuel. As Samuel heard the voice; he thought it to be Eli, so he answered; but Eli said, *"I didn't call you."* This continued three times in a row before Eli perceived that the Most High was calling Samuel. So, he said to Samuel, *"Go lie down and if you hear the voice again, say: "Speak Yahweh, for thy servant heareth."*

To be a 'Servant of Yahweh,' you must be willing to 'serve,' Him; in spite of anything else and above all else. By doing so, an obedient Servant will hear the Father speak. Are you listening, is the question, though or are we too busy with distractions. Samuel slept closely beside the Ark of Yahweh because he wanted to be in the presence of Him.

There was a time when I was so bombarded with things around me (the care of this life), whereas I couldn't hear my Father's voice... not even to give Him a few minutes of my time. I just kept right on doing my thing. Countless hours on the telephone, searching the internet for hours, catching up on the latest trends or daily dish of worldly gossip, watching Soap Operas. I was becoming like them, the "young and the restless." I was so restless until I could not hear the Father's speaking to me. Until something comes to pass, then I remembered, "Wow, if only I had listened to that 'still small voice, that spoke to me. No wonder, Psalms 46:10 left on record for us, *"Be still and know that I am Elohim; I will be exalted among the nations, I will be exalted in the earth."*

In order to hear, His voice, we must spend *alone* time with Him. I know I do. Sometimes, when I begin to hear His voice, I may not want to listen right then and there... but that is specifically the time that I must stop everything. Notice, it is our natural inclination, to respond angrily, *"WHAT?"* to someone, even when we do not want to be bothered; especially our children, when they call out our name, time after time, after time again!

But what I found out, in the Book of James' account, Chapter 1, verse 22, is that we are not to be *'hearers'* of the word *only* and not *'doers.'* We must stop, and attend to the cries of our children, just as we would want the Heavenly Father, to stop and attend to ours. He, too, knows if it is a cry of *hunger, pain or just plain ole' attention*. Otherwise, we can become off balance; and "*a just weight and balance, is of Yahweh, all the weights of the bag are His work*," Proverbs 16:11 reveals.

Samuel had a spiritually balanced life. He was indeed a '*hearer*' and a '*doer*,' for when the Father spoke to him, the first thing that came out of his mouth was, "*Here, I am, Father*,' not '*What*?!' Let's be like Samuel, let's start today, to hear with our spiritual ears, and not plug them as we do our natural ears.

The same applies to 'ME,' too, for I have learned to be still long enough (in a literal sense), to hear the Father's voice and say, "*Speak Father, thy Servant heareth*," with a response to obey, not to ask questions; but to receive direction to His command, and get busy doing what is asked of me. This takes some pressing, some real dedication to studying, fasting, praying and meditating.

Tune your spiritual ear to hear…. Are you listening? I'm Listening!

The Tip:
"With my whole heart have I sought thee;
O' let me not wander from thy Commandments."
Psalms 119:10

CHAPTER 21

+ ◆ ◆ ◆ +

There's No Place Like Home

It is now about 2:00 a.m., on a Thursday morning, and we are finally calming down from all the excitement of my being home. Wow! What a homecoming it was, I thought, as I laid between two Sisters... Yes, we were munched together in a queen-sized bed, and it felt so good lying next to them! It reminded me of being a child; having no choice but to sleep together. We talked for a few minutes and that was all I remembered until I woke up to use the rest room. I looked around for one of my Sisters, who was missing from out of the bed. I wandered through the house looking for her, and there she was in the other room, nestled under the cover of my best friend, who brought me. I must have been sleeping a little too wild. I stayed up, going over so many memories, in my mind while I sipped on a cup of coffee. I was overcome, knowing that Mama wasn't in the kitchen about to prepare a hot breakfast and there was no 'Daddy,' sitting on the front porch waiting to hear Mama call out: "*Honey, breakfast is ready,*" and all of us follow suit.

By now, everybody is '*up and at 'em,*' trying to get prepared for such a long day. A day of saying our 'goodbyes,' to our beloved Brother. It felt like a 'Sister's reunion, along with one of our Aunts. My one Sister, drove into the yard, with a big smile, "C'mon y'all, we got to take Globie shopping," as I wasn't allowed to leave the Camp with any of my own regular clothing, (*only the clothes, I was wearing*). Needless to say, I would need everything, *if you get my drift.* So off to the Mall, we went. Making haste.

Isn't that brilliant, how so much of our lives are already written for us, *"take no bags, no extra shirt, no shoes for your feet...,"* (Matthew 10:10, emphasis mine).

"Go ahead Sis, pick out whatever you want!" Such an enjoyable moment, that I was so ever grateful to be in; not to mention, I was like a kid in a candy store. I even felt like the Father, in the Book of Luke, where the Son returned home, and the Father brought forth the best of the best for him. I was blessed, to walk away, with the finest of things, that I needed to be presentable and some things that I wanted too. We serve the best Heavenly Fathers, and I was blessed with the best of Sisters. I was shown *favor*, spiritually and naturally! To say the least, I was overwhelmed with so much joy, that I began to cry. One of my precious Sisters said, *"It's okay, I know that if I was in your predicament, you would do the same for me."*

We were able to go the Funeral Home to view our Brother's body, before he was moved to the Church for the service. Oh, my goodness! I found myself in a state of shock; just seeing my Brother lying there. So many memories were traveling through my mind. I knew that my Brother fought a good fight; he finished his course and he kept the faith as Paul so plainly stated in 2nd Timothy 4:7-8. Yet, we were all still broken in sadness, naturally, as we left the Funeral Home.

I tried very hard, of course, not to be the center of attention, but it seemed as though I couldn't get around it. I was home, but wanted to grieve, but just as when *Mama* passed, and I was rendered helpless, to mourn, I wanted to go back to that place, clam up, not be sociable, but the real me, broke through. Just as I mentioned in previous Chapters, of the Menu, 'get to know the real you!' Because then, it wasn't a force, as I made myself available, for all of the laughter, hugs and kisses, and a few questions too, (*Wink, wink*).

We began to prepare ourselves for the Funeral, and yes, our home still sat 100 feet from the Church. We were surrounded by a lot of family and friends as well. *My oldest grandchild and my Nephew* were both my '*Knights in shining armour*,' making sure that I was holding up okay, *and that I was.... Until,* I viewed my Brother's body for the last time; I touched his cold hands, bent over and whispered, *"I will forever love you."*

Saying *goodbye* to a loved one, is one of the hardest things to ever do, in my opinion; knowing in the physical, you won't see them anymore. My heart was heavy as I walked away from the casket. I struggled to hold on to my '*Knights*,' as we gloried in a very moving and beautiful farewell. Singing wonderful songs which soothed our souls. I took in everything, all the scenery, and of course, glanced down the entire row, at my loved ones... "*Oh, how great, it felt being home with them.*" I smiled, as I tasted my salty tears that continued to flow from my eyes. Then, my Brother's casket was being rolled down the Church's aisle, one last time, being put into the hearse, by the Pallbearers, to go to its final resting place; I could not bare to go along with my other Sisters and Brothers, knowing that that's where loved ones were buried, whose funerals I was *unable* to attend. *Bitter Sweet*! But, I knew that I would need that time alone. Just as I did for my *beloved Husband*, when I went back later.

It's always a good thing, to know what you *can* and *cannot* handle, rather than allowing others to make those choices for you; ones that you regret later, all because you were too afraid to say, '*No thank you.*'

So, I stood in the Church's foyer with some of our other relatives, waiting until the family returned from the Cemetery, as well as friends, for the repast meal and fellowship. Hopeful to, one day soon, visit their gravesites. Back at the house, I just sat on the porch, relishing in the overwhelming joy; thankful for the blessings that the Heavenly Father bestowed upon me, just to be '*HOME.*'

The Tip:
"O' taste and see that Yahweh is good!"
Psalm 34:8

CHAPTER 22

✦✦✦✦

A Little Joy Goes A Long Way

Have you ever felt that all your "*joy*" was depleted? Do you know that you are in control of your own "*joy*?" Can you find "*joy*" in the smallest things? Will your "*joy*" ever be fulfilled in this life? These are just a few questions you must ask yourself from time to time; as I have had to do… because just having "*a little joy goes a long way!*"

Sometimes, when I counsel, meet or speak to people, one of the very first questions they want answered is… "*How can I be so joyful?*" (since I have been through so much) and maybe not as much as you or perhaps so much more; depending on your pomp of circumstances, as I am not declaring that I am the only one on this great planet that has suffered severe trials and tribulations; neither do I profess to be a '*know it all.*' But, there is one thing that I do know, *for sure*, and that is how I learned very valuable lessons within every situation.

People, however, are brutally honest, and do not bite their tongue, when after I admit what I've been through; goes further to ask… "*Am I now just ignoring the painful facts of life, and do not live in reality at all, because I remain humble and happy or am I just rather faking it.*" I simply respond, (which is true; since there's no way you can fake a bid in prison, no more than you can fake a pregnancy); yet I again, simply respond, that I am in no wise faking; just looking at difficulties from a different angle, in an attempt, to find the '*joy*' out of it all.

By the way, I do not have to look very far, to see where my Heavenly Father has brought me from. Neither do I have to put on a show, because I realized that it was *only* the Creator, that did not cause me to *become* miserable nor bitter, in the midst of life's challenges, to the point where I could have lost my mind, in which the enemy tried to destroy. If that is not *JOY*, you tell me what is! Even in the Gospel of John, he proclaims in Chapter 15 and verse 11, "*These things have I spoken to you, that My joy might remain in you, and that your joy might be full!*"

I embrace each day, that I am above ground and not six feet under, with '*joy*.' I am also reminded of the scripture, in Hebrews 12:15, "*Looking diligently lest any man fail of the grace of Elohim; lest any root of bitterness springing up trouble you; and thereby many be defiled.*"

Take advantage of every new day, with a fresh start. Trust in the Heavenly Father, Creator of the Universe, to do the rest. Think about yesterday as a 'cancelled check,' tomorrow as a 'promissory note,' and today as 'cash,' ready to spend on living! We do not have to worry about our future! Our life is in His hands, and every day is another opportunity given to do better, be better and get it together! Isn't that good to know?

As for me, I try not to let burdens paralyze my progress, and that progress is staying in His will. I have been given strength to look pass hurt and pains and lend a helping hand to others; who may be going through tough times, that I may bring joy unto them, which is also another example of fulfilling the Word from the book of 2nd Corinthians 1:4 to us, "Who comforts us in all our tribulations, that we may be able to comfort them which are in any trouble, by the comfort wherewith we ourselves are comforted of the Father."

Yes, there were and still are, many days and nights, I cry. We're human, yet I remain with a lasting '*joy*,' of a gentle and quiet spirit; knowing that "*they that sow in tears, shall reap in joy, He that goeth forth and weepeth, bearing precious seed, shall doubtless come again with rejoicing, bringing his sheaves with him.*" (Psalms 126:5-6) and how "*the joy of Yahweh is our strength,*" (Nehemiah 8:10)! Besides, haven't you heard that you are the only 'book,' a person may ever read. Therefore, never falter to let someone know, if the Father can restore your *JOY*, he can do the same for them.

I had a choice, as do you... To be miserable or to regain '*joy*.' Just know that the choice is yours! Job 8:21 proclaims, "*He has filled my mouth with laughter and my lips with shouts of joy."* Life is fragile, and every day is a gift. Live one day at a time, that is the secret that I have learned, and not only that, make right choices along the way for it *counts* towards *Eternity*, which awaits all of us.

The Tip:
"But the fruit of the spirit is love, JOY, peace,
Longsuffering, gentleness, goodness, faith!"
Galatians 5:22

CHAPTER 23

❖❖❖❖❖

Along Came Forgiveness

I was keeping a record, in my mind, of all the offenses from others. *Unforgiveness* had such a stronghold on me, that I had made *no intentions* about '*forgiving.*' I became just like the *Pharisees*: *preaching what is right to do but not practicing it myself.* And, I was not void of excuses, of what others had done to '*poor little ole' me!*' What was buried in my heart, had begun, at times, to spew out of my mouth. I thought for the longest that I *was* free. *Far from it!* I was being slowed down, in life, and in my walk, with the Heavenly Father; hurting no one but ME, MYSELF and I. *Have you been there… down the road of 'Unforgiveness?'*

Just in case you have not been down that lane, road or street… Let me inform you… *that harboring unforgiveness, in any way, shape, form or fashion, hurts you more than anyone else.* Unfortunately, I know from firsthand experience, that life is filled with injustices which can cause varying degrees of hurt and pain. Sometimes, it even made me feel that it was quite okay to hold on to it. I needed to be paid in full for the mental anguish that I endured. But as I was searching, "The Menu," (the Word), and just like that, out pops, *Ezekiel 11:19*, BAM! "*I will put a new spirit within them, and I will take the stony heart out of their flesh, and give them a heart of flesh.*"

Wow! I knew, right then and there, 'Along Came Forgiveness,' and I needed Yahweh to heal all those symptoms of 'unforgiveness!' I began to cry out to Him, for help. It was the perfect opportunity for me to let go of all the sentiments of unforgiveness that was bottled up within my heart and soul. *ONCE I BECAME HEALED, IT WAS EASY TO LET GO AND FORGIVE!*

The nerve of me... it's not my word that stands, but that of the Father, it says in Deuteronomy 32:55, "I will take vengeance, I will repay those who deserves it." Forgiveness taught me to move on with a real purpose; knowing that everything that had transpired in my life was destined to work out for my good; especially after I stop taking inventory of who, when, and where offenses came towards me, but turned it around to take inventory of MY sins, only mine, that the Creator has FORGIVEN me of.

The Tip:
"But there is forgiveness with thee!"
Psalm 130:4

CHAPTER 24

❖❖❖❖❖❖

From Rags to Righteousness

In the Thirty-fifth Chapter of Genesis, the Most High told His servant Jacob; arise and go to Bethel, dwell there and make an altar unto me. Jacob was an obedient servant. He said unto his household, and to all that was with him to put away the idols that were amongst them and be clean. Change your garments and let us arise and go up to Bethel. They brought unto him all of the idols and Jacob took and burned them.

Let me take you back to the Thirty-fourth Chapter of Genesis to recap what is going on… As Jacob and his household took their journey up to Bethel, they journeyed through the land of Canaan. He bought and pitched his tent within the City. His daughter, went out to see the daughters of the land. Shechem, the son of King Hamor, *saw, took, laid* and defiled her. He was in love with her, the Bible says. When Jacob heard what happened to his daughter, he was very angry, but he refrained from telling his sons. When he decided to tell his sons, they were very angry also; for this was shame brought to Israel, the Father's chosen people, from this uncircumcised man, who wanted to marry Jacob's daughter. After an agreement was made that all men be circumcised, so that they could become one with Jacob and his household, (but this was a trick).

Soon afterwards, all the men were sore from being circumcised and Jacob two sons, Simeon and Levi went in on the third day and killed all of them, including the King and his son. They took their Sister and spoiled the City, because of the evil that was done to their Sister. Now when Jacob heard about what his sons had done; he was angry with them. *"You have caused me to stink in the land of the Canaanites.*" Jacob was saying, that he had given people my word; for my word is all of me, because of this thing that you have done, will cause them to kill me and my household, which is very small in number. Jacob's sons were yet angry too, because of the way their Sister was dealt with, as though she was a harlot.

Jacob took the matter to the Most High in prayer. The Father answered him and said, 'Arise, and go up to Bethel. As their journey began, the Father protected them as they traveled through the Cities. The inhabitants of the Cities were afraid to pursue after them. Jacob and his household were under the protection of the Most High. Before taking their journey, all of the ruins and guilts were removed from amongst them. As you continue to read, you will see how the Father's blessing was upon Jacob; especially after Jacob got rid of the rags and continued to move in the righteousness of the Father.

Some years ago, I was in Los Angeles, California, teaching a class with the American International Hairweaving Association, and after a long day of working, a group of us decided to go sightseeing in Beverly Hills. Looking at all the beautiful homes, galleries and shops. Then, we later, decided to have dinner. As we were approaching this Diner; there laid beside the entrance, in a corner, a woman. She was all in rags. I said, 'Wow,' they are all over. As we were eating, the woman got us and passed by the window with her head down; engulfed in her sadness. A few days later, we went back to the same Diner... there I saw the lady again, but this time, she wasn't in rags. She was sitting at a table in the Diner, wearing beautiful, clean clothing; talking and laughing, surrounded by people.

I never knew the moral of the story, but when I see people walking around in rags, I often think about her; seeing that she cleaned herself up. 'Why can't we?' Keep in mind, I am talking about the physical rags, which are torn and dirty clothes that people can easily take off and clean themselves up. 'What about the mental rags?' The ruins and guilts that one carries around; keeping them from becoming righteous. These type of '*rags*' are heavier to carry and can easily weigh you down *spiritually*.

I know a lot about rags... I wore them for many years. I wore all kind of rags; rags of anger, rags of depression, rags of unforgiveness, hurt, bitterness, shame, fear, sickness and disparity. For a long time, I kept them 'undercover,' they were holding me in bondage, until they became too heavy for me to bear. So, just as Jacob told his household, change your garments, in other words, get rid of all the ruins and guilts. Notice, that I am not taking ownership by saying my rags, because ownership is something you get to keep, and I don't want to keep wearing rags. Again, I cried out to the Most High, and He heard my cry. I began to trust Him, and he began moving the rags from me, piece by piece. It wasn't an overnight process, not that the Father can't do it overnight; for He can do all things, whenever and however He wants to. (*"There is nothing too hard for Him,"* Jeremiah 32:27)! He takes His time, because He doesn't want your heart to be lifted up forgetting where He brought you from, (Deuteronomy 8:14).

I know everybody have worn some type of rags. They may not be the same as mine, but we all can wear, Job 29:14, *"He put on righteousness and it clothed him."* This is why, everywhere I had to go; no hurt, nor harm came near me. *Why?* I was clothed in righteousness not rags!

The Tip:
"I will greatly rejoice in my Father; my soul shall
be joyful unto Him, for He has clothed me with the
garment of salvation and has covered me
with the Robe of Righteousness."
Isaiah 61:10

TO

GO

PLATES

CHAPTER 25

+ ◆ ◆ ◆ ◆ +

A Weeping Widow

A s I stated in earlier Chapters of "*The Menu*," I was born into a large family. There were six *gals* and three *knucklehead* boys. (Three older Sisters, then two older Brothers and then there were the rest of us. I was in the middle with two Sisters and a Brother under me). My three oldest Sisters took very good care of the three youngest Sisters, as *Daddy* and *Mama* went off to work. The oldest Sisters were *always* in charge of taking care of the house, also.

There came a time when my oldest Sisters graduated and left home to start a life of their own. I remembered thinking that *Washington, D.C* and *New York*, seemed like it was so very far away, when I was a child and probably because for a long time, I didn't see them for a long time. I, in turn, had to step in and be a big Sister to my younger siblings; which meant taking care of them, like my older Sisters had done unto me. When we played house, I always took on the role as "*Momma.*" Everybody had to listen to me! It was fun, most of the time, until they wouldn't agree with me), on how to run the house or follow the 'Leader.' Isn't that typical of us with the Heavenly Father, all is well until we decide to go contrary; then we want to leave *His* house (The Church) but 1ˢᵗ Peter 4:17-18, is right there, slap, dab in the middle to remind us, "*For the time is come that judgment must begin at the house of Elohim; and if it first begin at us, what shall the end be of them that obey not the gospel of Elohim? And if the righteous scarcely be saved, where shall the ungodly and the sinner appear?*"

Well, for that reason, of wanting to lead my younger siblings, I was teased a lot about having a '*Widow's Peak.*" What is a '*Widow's Peak?*' some may ask…

A *Widow's Peak* is the hair that grows from the top of your head towards the center of your forehead, forming a V-shape downward. Much like an old television show called, "*The Monster,*" that featured a little boy who also had one. My siblings would go on further to *tease* me and say things like: *When I grow up and get married, my Husband was going to die or leave me for another woman*, because of my *Widow's Peak*. My, oh my, how fearful was that to think about as a child? So, every chance I got… I would ease into the bathroom and use Daddy's razor to shave the *Widow's Peak*. The more I shaved, the thicker it became. Daddy began to notice how someone had been using his razor, leaving hair behind, no less. He knew it wasn't my *Brothers*, because they were too young to have facial hair. So, he inquired about it; yet with no response *from me*. That's me today, that was Jonah back then, and so many countless others, we dare to respond, however, Psalm 53:2 does it for us, "*Elohim looked down from heaven upon the children of men, to see if there were any that did understand, that did seek Elohim.*"

So, just as our Creator does when He is not finished with us; Daddy sought me out. He needed only to *LOOK* at *ME*, and that's when he saw that there wasn't any hair growing on my forehead. I had to stop using Daddy's razor. *Now what was I to do?* My hair began to grow even the more. Just call me that ole' "*Weeping Willow*" tree we talked about in the earlier Chapters; that was in our beautiful yard. During the long summer days, my siblings and I, alike, all played in the backyard. We would watch our *Parents* as they sat under the "*Weeping Willow*" tree talking and laughing with one another. They could name every flower, tree and plant! The "*Weeping Willow*" tree, was a tree that was so very beautiful during the day, but as the sun would begin to set, and the sky darken, the leaves would begin to wilt, causing the tree to look as if it was "*weeping.*"

As time passed, I met and fell in love with a man who *became my Husband*. He began to admire my beauty; *ESPECIALLY*, my '*Widow's Peak.*' He told me it was different; yet so beautiful. (One of the many things that attracted him to me, he'd then tease). So certainly, what my Sister's said about my '*Widow's Peak,*' was thrown out of the window like as a pail of water. *It didn't matter ANYMORE... I even began to just LET IT GROW!*

Thirty-two years later, my Husband and I was visiting one of our Sons; (both lived about twenty minutes away from one another). But this day, my Husband stayed at the one Son's home, while I left to attend my Cousin's funeral. Afterwards, I called that I'd get us some dinner on the way back, but did not hang up the telephone until we expressed how much we loved each other.

As I headed towards my Son's house, I began watching the sun as it began to set and I also sped up a little, hoping I could make it to my Husband, so we could watch the setting of the sun together, which we loved *to do.* The sun was just over the horizon, when I approached my Son's house, so I immediately ran, excitedly towards the door, and stopped in my tracks, when I noticed my Husband lying on the porch. I said, "*Jimi, Why are you lying down like that?!*" But he didn't answer. I said, "*WAKE UP, JIMI, WAKE UP!*" Still no answer. I then touched him, and he didn't move. I began to cry, running at the same time, to get help. Words of "*HELP ME,*" forming in my brain, but not coming out of my mouth. So, as the sun set... as it did on the "*Weeping Willow*" tree, in our backyard, many years ago, and just as I had been *teased* by my Sister's about becoming a '*Widow,*' (they didn't know, of course), yet, it came to pass.

With the setting of the sun, *September 16, 2007,* I became a "*Weeping Widow.*"

The Tip:
"To everything there is a season, and a time to
every purpose under the heaven....
A time to 'weep' and a time to laugh."
Ecclesiastes 3:1, 4

CHAPTER 26

✦✦✦✦✦

Speak Life

Already in a depressive state of mind, watching my Husband battle that vicious disease called, 'Pancreatic Cancer, I became worse as the days surpassed, after his demise. It took everything out of me. I lacked energy, on a daily basis, spending most of my time in bed; trying to sleep away the haunting pain of losing someone, so dear. I didn't realize, in all actuality, I was developing physical illness due to the adverse emotions. I became toxic! It was tearing me down, day by day… physically, psychologically and spiritually. There was this tremendous fear of being alone coupled with inadequacies, and rightly so… this was my LIFE PARTNER! I began to lose my desire to live. I grew tired of even my lips tasting the salty tears, as they ran down my cheeks. At the rate I was plummeting; there wouldn't be any more bottles to bottle up any one else tears for my Heavenly Father. To make matters worse, I was dragging my two Sons into the death trap with me. They tried their best to comfort me, as I was grieving, when I forgot, they too were grieving from the loss of their great 'Dad.'

Chronic illnesses kicked in high gear, stopping at nothing til I be destroyed. I was suffering from all sorts of ailments. Mainly, an 'Incisional Hernia,' that kept me, constantly, in and out of the hospital, with corrective surgeries. During each surgical interval… which they weren't too far apart, I was getting sicker. I was losing strength due to the internal bleeding and if I wanted to live, I would have to make a complete 'U-turn!' Nurses were assigned to my home even; as I was too ill to leave the house.

If you are ever confronted with a 'life or death,' situation, your whole perspective in life will deepen! And if you are surrounded by family and people that 'truly' love you... you just may might make it. That is how it happened for me... It was something that one of my Sons said... I will never forget it... as it is etched in my mind, heart and soul.

I was visiting them after being out of the hospital for three weeks; in his home. I looked like a pregnant woman and I was very weak, still bleeding internally too; trying to hide the way I was feeling and looking. But this day, my Daughter-in-Law knocked on the bedroom door, and before I could tell her to come in; she opened the door and there I stood, trying desperately to cover my swollen stomach. She pretended as if she didn't see it. We had a brief conversation and then she left the out of the bedroom and went crying to my Son, (a Daughter-in-Law, after my own heart, who didn't even grow up in the 'Tell-It-All-Neighborhood). Well, she told him that day... that something was *'wrong with me.'*

He came and sat on the floor beside the bed, teared up but spoke ever so humble and strong, *"Now Momma,"* he said, *"Every since I've known you... you have been a praying Woman and a good Mother to me and my Brother, and the most beautiful thing about your prayers is that God always answered them; especially concerning anything about us; your Sons. It took us years to figure out... how you knew when something was troubling us or that we were in trouble. Now Momma, it's only been a couple of months since Daddy passed, please Momma don't have us go through losing our last parent."* He continued, *"I know without a doubt, if you will find the strength to pray, and ask for healing, God will answer you... He always does, Momma!"*

That conversation was the straw, as they say, that broke the camel's back. I became a self-motivator; *empowering myself,* spiritually with plenty of *'Appetizers* (Prayers),' eating daily from *'The Menu,'* and I began to "SPEAK LIFE," and not death. I beseeched the Father, that He would give me the 'will to live, and not die. I knew that He was able to do more than I could even ask or ever imagine, just like He said in Ephesians 3:20, (read it for yourself). HE HADN'T MOVED... I DID!

In *Him,* I was safe, although death was hovering around me. The Father knew my fears, was counting up my tears, and was going to give me the strength to FIGHT. I started gaining spiritual weight and had to continue to ask the Father for what I needed and not confine Him to limited resources. There wasn't any room to be afraid. I was determined not to put all of those chemicals (medications), into my body, as I saw how it affected my Husband, '*healing one thing and damaging another.*' Every Doctor's appointment that I had; he would prescribe a pain medication, which I would never take. There was this one thing that I did know, and that was what I needed to do... which was totally rely on my Heavenly Father for healing because He told me in Malachi 4:2, "*Unto him that fear my name, shall the sun of righteousness arise with healing in his wings, and ye shall go forth as the calf of the stall.*"

I became a 'Warrior," on a spiritual battlefield. I prayed daily for health restoration and His permission for me to LIVE. And the healing began! My Sons were so excited to witness such a miraculous comeback and gloated, "*See, I told you, there has never been a time when Momma's prayers weren't answered,*" my one Son shouted to his Brother.

A few months later, I received a letter in the mail. It was a scheduled appointment, for me to visit my Doctor. When the time came, and I went for my '*check-up,*' even the Doctor was astounded, to see such a great improvement. He shared that his concern for me was so intense, because I was knocking at death's door. I replied with a smile, "*My faith brought me through,* and he said, "*Keep believing!*"

The Tip:
"*For thus saith Yahweh, unto the House of Israel*
Seek ye me, and ye shall live."
Amos 5:4

CHAPTER 27

◆◆◆◆◆

Who Is It?

Shortly after the deaths of my two *loves, my Husband,* and *my Daddy,* I began to feel so overwhelmed, like the world was coming to an end. The years of the love combined, UNFATHOMABLE! We cherished great *'enlightments'* about life with much joy and laughter. *Oh, how I miss them both*!

Anxiety zapped my energy and I began to lose control of my mind *and* who I was. I became very depressed and crazy thoughts stole my last moments of consciousness, invading the privacy of my mind, before falling asleep, *most nights*. Instead of feeding myself from *'The Menu,'* (the *'Word'*), to gain spiritual strength, I turned to prescribed medications again, such as *pain killers, antidepressants, and anything else* that would keep my mind *cloudy*, in the midst of my *'storm,'* to try to relieve the emotional pain that gripped me yet again. I was riding a roller coaster, that was taking me deeper and deeper into an abyss of *'nothingness,'* and all I wanted to do was just drown in sadness. I slipped and fell and did not adhere to the nutrients that was being supplied. That's when Proverbs 26:14 played out, *"where a just (righteous) man falleth seven times but he gets up and go for it again; never giving up the fight."*

One night, deep in the depth of my soul, a voice kept rising up, saying, "You can have peace, joy and your happiness back... all you need to do is place an *'Order,'* from *'The Menu,'* (*The Word*). Which is how this book was brought into fruition.

Again, I had to spiritual self-medicate myself... *"You already know all* the different 'meals,' (Scriptures), that are available to you; and if you're not totally ready to 'order,' just start with some 'Appetizers,' (Prayers) which will lead and direct you to what you need." I listened to my *inner man*, and it wasn't long before my *peace, joy and happiness* showed back up, with the help of Isaiah 26:3, *"He that keepeth his mind stayed on thee, will keep him in perfect peace, because he trusts in thee.* I was able to kick all the medications to the curb! But the two key principles, however, is to *keep* your mind *'stayed on him'*, and the part we forget, and to *'trust in him.'* "KEEP, STAY AND TRUST."

It was a busy day, when my *keep, stay and trust*, reservoir was low, to when an old visitor came knocking *at the door of my mind. KNOCK, KNOCK, KNOCK*! I tried so hard to focus and not answer. Fear began to show its ugly face again; so, I answered, *"Who Is It?"* It said, *"It's me!"* I replied, *"Who Is Me?"*

"You know who it is, It's Me, 'Sadness.' Stop playing and let me come in… I haven't heard from you, in a while. I only want to entertain you. I know that you have been missing me; trying so hard to fight and escape the pain that is throbbing throughout that pretty little head of yours. I promise if you will let me come in for a short visit, I will comfort you with what you need." Well, why fight the feeling of a few doses of *'Trazadone*, and maybe a little *'Prozac,'* and *'Zoloft'* too, for desert,' to ease this conversation and my troublesome mind all at once. *A Cocktail! Sounded good to me, Umpf!*

Then, the Heavenly Father would begin to strengthen me, whenever I became weak, *'for when I am weak, then am I strong,'* giving me the boldness to *'gird up the loins of my mind'* and fight against that thing called "*fear,*" which was just an illusion dancing within my head. So when that knock came, and the unwanted visitor appeared, I replied, *"No, Sadness, I can't let you come in. You see, I don't need you anymore!"*

I had a *"GET THEE BEHIND ME,"* moment… you know the moment… when the Heavenly Father was likewise tempted in Matthew, Chapter 4, when *'he was led up of the Spirit into the wilderness to be tempted of the devil,'* and *'offered him all the kingdoms in the moment of a time,'* verses one through eleven.

Every so often, I would have thoughts, *"You can run but you can't hide; I will destroy your "freedom" of thought or I will control you wherever you go… I have a dependency on you; you can't escape!"* But, I paraphrase here, that, "Greater is He that is in me, than he that is in my mind," and NO SADNESS can penetrate to the point where I am dependent on controlled substances, because only faith is the substance! I have regained my mental faculties back through indulging in a plethora of appetizers and from ordering everything from 'The Menu,' (the Word), that I need. I've been redeemed.

Who's knocking at your door, unexpectedly? And when you respond, "*Who Is It?*" Who will be on the other end? Here is the answer....

"*Behold, I stand at the door and knock, if man hear My voice and open the door, I will come in to him and will sup with him and he with Me.*"

And now when I get a knock at the door, and I respond, "*Who Is It?*" It says, "*Happiness,*" *peace spread with a topping of joy!*"

The Tip:
"*The Father has not given a spirit of fear;*
But of power, love and a sound mind."
2ⁿᵈ Timothy 1:7

CHAPTER 28

✦ ✦ ✦ ✦ ✦

The Blessed Captivity

There was a Prophet of the Most High, in the Bible, by the name of Jeremiah. He wrote to all of those that were carried away into captivity by the Babylonian King. Jeremiah, Chapter 29 said, "Listen, these are the words of the Most High Creator of Israel; I have allowed you to be captured; but I am going to allow you to prosper, in your captivity. This is what I want you to do: I want you to build houses and live in them… Plant gardens and eat from them… Take you wives, and have sons and daughters to husbands, that they may bear sons and daughters.

Jeremiah told them to do all of this while being in captivity that they may increase there and not be diminished, (Verse 6). This reminds me of the seventy souls that went down to Egypt, and a nation was birthed from these seventy souls (Israel). Keep in mind, it was just a residue of Israel that was taken into captivity from Jerusalem. Then he told them that the Father told them to seek the peace of the City that have been cursed, then to be captured. Then I want you to pray unto the Father for it; for in the peace thereof, you shall have peace! Jeremiah continues to read the letter, telling the that the Father said, after being in captivity for seventy years, I am coming back to visit, and I am going to perform my good word. It never ceases to amaze me the things that He will do for His children. For He says, Verse 11-13, "*I know my thoughts that I think towards you.*" He said that "*they are thoughts of peace and not of evil; to give you an expectant end. Then shall you call upon me and pray unto me and I'll hearken unto you. And you shall seek Me, and find Me, when you shall search for Me with all your heart.*" As you meditate on this letter that Jeremiah read to the Children of Israel; ask yourself the question, *'Are you blessed in captivity?'*

As a Servant of the Most High, I was blessed while I was being held in a Babylon City. While being in captivity, I persevered, endured hardness, and most of all; I trusted in the Father, to direct my path and to strengthen me. While I was helping and showing my people how to become sovereign, I was faced with great troubles; that weakened me physically, but my spirit man was at PEACE! No matter what I was going through, I was trusting Yahweh. One of my favorite sayings is, "*If the Father brought me to it; He'll see me through it.*"

The Children of Judah was also in captivity, (Verse 22), and I blessed them, for they are my chosen ones, just as you are my Servant says the Father, and the Father said to me as He said unto Judah; '*While you are still being held in captivity, this is what I want you to do; my assignment was to go in and pull up the women that are torn down, tell of the goodness of Me to the broken-hearted, be a light in the darkness and seek the peace of the City that have you captive; and pray unto me for it.*' Now the Father was doing okay, until He told me to seek and pray for the City that held me captive. Did I want to pray for the City that held me captive? NO! I said to the Creator, '*Listen, Father, let's talk about this thing…*' *Do you really want me to seek peace and to pray for the City that took me captive?* You see, you have to talk to the Creator, as you do a natural man… Be honest. Talk to Him in the realm of the spirit and through 'The Menu,' (the Word). Yahweh continued to still speak with me, saying, '*After you have accomplished the work that I have sent you to do; I'm coming back to visit you, and when I do… I am going to perform my good word toward you and cause you to be set free.*

Isaiah 50:4 says, "*He has given me the tongue of the learned, that I may know how to speak a word in season to them that is weary.*" And because of the 'blessed captivity,' I have the testimony of Joseph, "What was meant to harm me, my Father turned it around for my good!

The Tip:
"Blessed be Yahweh, for He has shown me His
marvelous kindness in a strong City."
Psalms 31:21

CHAPTER 29

✦ ✦ ✦ ✦ ✦

Thy Sister's Keeper

As we gathered for our Tuesday morning class, to discuss our weekend, everyone came with big smiles. I assumed everybody had a visit or was able to talk to their family. I believed that my smile was the biggest and I couldn't tell why, since out of four, I would be the last one to share. Lately, I noticed, how the Most High had really been manifesting His greatness in not only my situation, but my LIFE.

I was finally able to share how I was able to speak with one of my Sisters, who I had not spoken with in over two years; and all I needed to do for this to happen, was to practice '*Exodus 14*' which instructed me to '*stand still and see His salvation.*' This particular Chapter describes how the Most High tells Moses to *tell his people the Israelites*, not to fear, but to stand and see His salvation. This is after Moses led them out of Egypt, and Pharaoh and his Army was in pursuit of them. So, I am learning to follow His instructions. Also, thanks to a Cousin and a Best Friend, they made the phone call possible.

When we first heard one another's voices, my Sister and I, we both, naturally began to cry. Then started to thank and praise the Father for His goodness and mercy toward us.

This Sister, was the '*Protector*,' of the family, and oh so comical; the joy! Never a dull moment, because she could uplift the dullest of spirits, and it was infectious. You couldn't even stop laughing once she got started; especially in school, when we were kids. But she could be serious too, if someone was bullying any one of us! She even gave my *boyfriend* (who later became my Husband), a run for his money also; they were always going at it. I was so glad when they became friends! I want to attribute that to the comic in *the both of them*, or he was afraid of her, as he witnessed firsthand how bold she was in defending me in our High School years, so he knew he had better treat me like GOLD, (which he did).

In my review of the fourth Chapter of the Book of Genesis, Yahweh asked Cain; "*Where is thy brother?*" Cain answered, by saying, "*I don't know*," and in the same breath, asked the Father, "*Do I look like my Brother's keeper?*" Cain was very bold, wasn't he? The nerve of him to ask the Creator of the Universe, such a question. If the Father would have asked me, where was my Sister, the one I had the opportunity to speak with that day, I would have answered, "*I don't know, at the moment, but I do know that* "*SHE IS MY KEEPER!*" She kept me '*sane*,' and laughing after the deaths of our Dad, and after the death of my Husband. Also, we would spend a lot of time together, along with our other Sisters, even though we lived in different States, but nevertheless, it was such a highlight; whenever we all were able to be in one another's presence.

I remember going to see my Sister, one time, just because, I was led. Always follow your first mind. The visit was surreal, because as I went to see her, I learned that she had been hospitalized. I rushed to the hospital to check on her, and thank goodness, she was being released, and I was able to help her home. That was one of those precious moments, when I made my famous homemade soup; hoping that that would make her feel better. Her Husband was happy to be a benefactor of some of his favorite dishes too. I love my family and -my Brother-in-Laws! We don't have to stop at being our *Brother or Sisters keeper*, we can be a *Family keeper*! I may have to give up, to all of them, my secret recipes after all, (Fried cabbage and my good ole' fried chicken being their favorite).

As the evening progressed, when we brought my Sister home from the hospital; everyone was tucked in for the night, and I was in the guest bedroom reading. There was a knock at the door. It was my Sister, with her pillow, coming to lay across the bed with me; *sick*, but still willing to talk, and make sure that I was okay. As we were talking, she told me to, '*be quiet*,' because she heard something. She peeked out the window and saw nothing. So, we continued to talk. Then came a louder knock on the door... she got up to answer it. Taking too long to return, I went to see what was going on… not knowing this moment would change my whole life.

The Tip:
"Behold, He that keepeth Israel shall neither
slumber nor sleep. The Most High is Thy Keeper."
Psalms 121:4-5

CHAPTER 30

You Can Run; But
You Can't Hide

The Creator knows all and sees all! There was no way, I could hide or run from Him now. I was in Jonah's shoes, with a resistant heart and running in the opposite direction. I was at the stance of Hezekiah, turning my face to the wall, in lamentations, crying and praying. And I had suffered like Job, and just wanted to die. I was locked away, and later found out, within my that I wasn't locked away, I was *'tucked,'* away, *for my own good.*

After the big explosion, everybody, *including myself,* was in a state of shock. A state of unbelief of my arrest. I didn't know where to turn. I felt helpless. I knew that I would have to trust in the Father, and that He would not let me be put to shame, or at least that was my prayer. My pity party lasted for quite some time, as I was in a cold cell, all alone, initially. Until I had a light bulb moment, I really wasn't ALL alone.

The Most High's presence was *'with me.'* You see, once He *'catches,'* up with you, and get your attention, He is able to manifest His greatness unto you. Psalm 73:28, I found helpful, as well, *"But it is good for me to draw near to Yahweh; I have put my trust in Him, that I may declare all thy works."*

YOU CAN RUN, BUT YOU CAN'T HIDE! Even when you try to flee from His presence. He is still constantly guiding, directing, caring and watching over His children. "Yahweh will not forsake His people, for His great name's sake, for it pleases Him to call you His people," (1st Samuel 12:22)

The Tip:
"Thy word have I hid in my heart; that I might
not sin against thee."
Psalms 119:11

CHAPTER 31

He's Always There

The relationship between my Heavenly Father and I have become closer and closer. It has become "*fortified*" even. I would not have been able to endure the trials nor any future difficulties that may arise without Him. I can truly say that He rescued me from every evil work that came against me. Perhaps you have experienced distressing circumstances or difficult situations as well and felt all alone in dealing with them. *That was me!* I was to the point, where I was disappointed by not receiving assistance from people, when I asked. That's when I realized that my problems couldn't be solved by *human* help.

Rather than nurture resentment; when human help appeared to be limited, I viewed the situation as an opportunity to fully rely on the Creator of the Universe. I was able to experience *firsthand*, that "*He's Always There!*" His loving care and constant protection was beyond measure. I read in 1st Corinthians 10:13, that "*He will not allow me to suffer beyond my limit of endurance*," and Yes, He is a 'Way-Maker, "*for He always makes a way out.*"

I looked at my trials as being on the training ground to become a powerful Soldier (Servant) for Yahweh. *Ask me why I feel this way?* Because people are looking for a strong person that can help them; to lead and guide them through pressing situations, so with great humbleness, I make myself readily available *to* help.

I think about Psalms 106:6 which says, "*I will keep a protective eye on the righteous, so they may dwell with me in safety.*" Therefore, it does not matter where I am... I have the assurance that I am in safety *and so are you*! Just continue to hold on to the faith of Yahweh and hand over your troubles to Him. He is always willing and able to make everything alright, because at the end of the day, HE'S ALWAYS THERE!

The Tip:
"Happy is the man who keeps on enduring trials,
Because on becoming approved; he will receive the crown of life."
James 1:12

CHAPTER 32

✦✦✦✦

Blessings In Disguise

At times in our lives, there may be circumstances that come our way, that may make us think we have lost, or may lose our mind; but really, in the end, WE LOSE NOTHING! (Read John 6:37-39). It doesn't matter what you are going through or what you have been through; just so long as you do not *give up* along the way. I know for a surety, that the Father answer '*prayers.*' Even when I'm doubtful of what I ask of Him.

It had been months, since I had been able to see my *Boys*; and how I worried, as I know they did as well, *about me.* My mind raced, '*Where are they? What are they doing? Are they taking care of themselves? Will I ever see them again?*' You see, truth be told, as I was being flown back from the Airport, to find out my fate; I had just discovered the fate of my two Sons. *Frightening* was an understatement. I fought long and hard, day and night, for them, in an injustice *Justice* system, where extremely long sentences were given, for the very things, they figured out in the 21st Century that does not warrant that kind of punishment. But, there is one thing I do know, and that is things happen in our lives that cause us to lose, in order to gain.

I continued to pray; because the Father, is '*a present help in the time of trouble,*' and He is just waiting for us to *seek His face*; to give Him praise and thanksgiving, for bringing us out. And not only when we are faced with unsurmountable issues, but just for HIS breath of life. Without Him, we literally, can do nothing, (John 15:5), no matter how much we try. He is the vine and the branches, I needed to stop going out on a limb!

As the flight continued, I *continued* fast in prayer. I was praying that the Father help me to be able to accept whatever His will may be for my family as well as myself. Afterall, it was *our* bad choices, at that time, that caused the predicament. And although, I never lost my hope, in knowing, that the Father will always rescue those that are His; I also knew that '*a curse won't come causeless,*' Proverbs 26:2 tell us that, "*As the bird by wandering, as the swallow by flying, so the curse causeless shall not come.*" So, I became reassured as I packed up all of my hurt, pain *and* the pride that came along with it and placed them into the Father's hand, closed and rested my eyes, before the next stop; which was at the *Atlanta* Airport. *I felt like Abraham, fleeing to a City, not knowing where I'd end up.*

I sat in my seat, staring out of the window, *waiting*, as the Officers began to call passengers, one by one, to exit the airplane. I didn't have a clue, one way or the other, if I would be called at all, but prayed just the same, that I *would be*; and since speaking with my Daughter-in-Law, some weeks earlier, I just wanted off; as it was a possibility that my sons were somewhere at a holding facility in *Georgia*. '*If only, I could see them or hear their voices,*' although, I knew deep within that they would be okay; because remember, I gave *EVERYTHING* over to the Father. I couldn't carry it... He told me I didn't have to carry it, and I refused to carry it. I was far from a 'bag lady and by now, you also know, *what* I chose to eat from off '*The Menu*' (*the Word*), as a treat... Yes, 1ˢᵗ *Peter 5:7*, "*Cast our care,*" not carry our care, "*upon Him, for He careth for us.*" (Emphasis mine). I had to free myself, first, at this juncture, so I could save them later.

So, my *name*, which was actually a *number* now, sounded, *85051332*! "*Oh, my goodness, that's me. For a moment, I forgot that I would not hear my name, for a while, but would have to answer to a Federal number, and not your social security number either, try getting use to that... NO... DON'T TRY!*" I jumped up, thinking, "*Yes, A BLESSING IN DISGUISE! I am getting off of this plane! Bound in shackles and all,*" although it took me a few minutes to actually move. I had to give the blood time to recirculate within my legs from sitting so long without the liberty to stretch. Now, as I walked across the gate, out to a yard, to a van that was waiting, I turned into 'Hannah,' praising and thanking the Father, with my lips, without voice: "*Thank you for your divine protection, for you have once again showed me your awesome power, and your wonderous works, and for that, I will not fear mortal man."*

When I approached the van, I was told to wait at the side door until some other people were removed from it, to board the plane, that I had just exited from. The Driver came up to me, and for some strange reason, asked me my *'Government name,'* at least three times over. I wanted to say, *'You already have the Government number, leave me alone.'* Of course, you had to use whatever scruples, you had, and just answer; while at the same time, stay mindful to *"Be not forgetful to entertain strangers, for thereby, some have entertained angels unawares,"* (Hebrews 13:2). There was another woman, standing beside me, wondering why they kept asking. Her guess was good as mine. We used our eyes to communicate.

Finally, the people started exiting the van, single file. I heard a *'voice,'* and thought I was dreaming. *"Hey Momma! I LOVE YOU!"* I reached for him, out of instinct, my Son, but he was pulled away. I began to cry. *"Don't you dare let them break you! I LOVE YOU MOMMA!*

There was a period of time, in my life, that I didn't believe in my own self. I would pray, but still had many doubts; that the Father could ever bring me out! Boy, did he show me this day… and while our circumstances may seem to make no sense to us or to those around us, and sometimes we can't see any way out of our mess, let me encourage you… just like it is written in Hebrews 12:11, *"No chastening for the present seems joyous; but grievous,"* and I was happy and sad at the same time, *"nevertheless afterward it yields the peaceable fruit of righteousness to them which are exercised thereby,"* seek the peace of the Father. Let Him become your refuge and strength, when you feel hopeless, and allow Him to work His miraculous plan, right before your very eyes.

The Tip:
"In my distress, I call on the Father. I cry to Him for help.
From His temple, He heard my voice; my cry came before Him,
into His ears; and then He turns around and bring me out
into a spacious place; He rescued me because He delights in me."
Psalm 18:6, 19

CHAPTER 33

✦✦✦✦

The Strong Will Survive

I had to '*act*,' with strength and courage, no matter how I was feeling or what I was thinking at this point in time. I had to use, what I deemed as three of the most powerful words, in the English language, "*JUST DO IT!*" I kept telling the Most High, '*I trust you*,' but did I?

If I was going to survive, I would have to get fully dressed into my battle clothes, *the sword of the spirit, the shield of faith, the breastplate of righteousness, the helmet of salvation and the shoes of readiness*. It was time to get off the '*pity pot*,' and get spiritually busy. T hat's when I wrote a letter to my '*Heavenly Father*.'

Dear Father:

I rejoice in you for you are my peace (shalom), and I will forever worship you. At this present moment, I feel like a caged bird, whose wings have been clipped, causing me not to be able to fly. I need you to lead and guide. My heart is plummeting out of control and I can't even follow a thought. Please Father, continue to hide me under your wings for there, I know I am safe. Speak to me that I may hear you. I need you more than I have ever needed you before; so go ahead, and have your way. The door to my heart is wide opened. Speak loud, Father, so that I can hear you, for right now, my hearing is a little cloudy. O' Father, do not keep silent, be not quiet, and O' Father, be not still.

After that, my Heavenly Father, calmed my mind. I was no longer in abandonment; asking Him, '*Where are you*? For I knew that He was near. I developed an even deeper hunger for His word and guidance. And as I was about to open '*The Menu*,' (the Word), my action, of picking up my Bible to read, was interrupted by a note someone slid under my door. I picked up the piece of paper, opened it, and there was, "*Isaiah 41:10-13*," written on it; without a deliverer's name; though I knew who it was from.... my '*Ultimate Deliverer*,' and from that moment forward, I never compromised my faithfulness in serving my Heavenly Father, Creator and King of the Universe; nor was I ashamed to proclaim His holy and righteous word, with boldness; for it was because of His '*Word*,' I received hope and it was because of His '*Word*," I had been taught *how to survive* with a '*strong will*.'

The Tip:
"Behold, all they who enrage and inflame against you shall
be put to shame and confounded; they that strive against you
shall be as nothing and perish."
Isaiah 41:11

CHAPTER 34

A Dove Messenger

When the floodgates of the sky burst opened, the rain fell on the earth, forty days and forty nights. Scripture tells us that Noah and his family, along with all the beast of every kind were on the Ark, when the flood began. (Genesis 7:11-12).

At the end of the forty days of raining, Noah sent out a raven *to and fro* until the waters had dried up from the earth. Then he sent a dove to see whether the water had decreased from the surface of the ground. The dove returned because it could not find a resting place for its feet. Seven days later, he sent the dove out again. The dove came back to him and there in its bill was a plucked off olive leaf. Noah waited another seven days and sent the dove out again… this time, the dove didn't return to him anymore.

It amazing how the Most High used something as small as a dove to deliver a message. Just think, He is yet using doves to bring forth messages, as one was delivered to me. It came as I sat talking, in a deep conversation, with one of my roommates, about having faith and trusting our Heavenly Father, to work out every detail in our lives; whether it be great or small. I expressed how I had to trust the Father to move on my behalf to send me closer to home. I did not get to see my family, where I was; and there was nothing like being able to embrace your love ones. She added an, 'AMEN,' to that, and there were many other days, where we just sat and cried and laughed amongst one another, just to make it through the day. I was told that I was eligible to be furloughed to a 'Camp,' of my choice. Of course, you already know that I chose one that was within six hours from my hometown. Oh boy, I sure did rejoice!

As the months kept passing me by; I kept waiting for someone to tell me, "It's time to go!" People were leaving every day and I just couldn't understand why I was being overlooked. I told my roommate, that I have been planning for months, and how I've acted responsibly; that I wasn't going to fret… I would just lay back and trust the Most High for the results. Sometimes, I would get anxious about decisions, quite naturally now, that would affect my future, therefore, I had to remain calm. *"Be careful for nothing,"* Phillipians 4:6 states, *"but in everything by prayer and supplication with thanksgiving, let your requests be made known to the Father."* Therefore, I had to remain steadfast in my walk of faith, and let the Father instruct me and most of all teach me, in the way I should go.

So, we sat in the stillness of the moment, starring out of the window; letting our words take root in our minds and there came, out of nowhere, a dove to the window; just pecking, fiercely too, as if it was trying to get into our room. We sat in reverence, at such a profound moment. And within that instance, my name was being called to report to the Secretary's office. I stood up to go downstairs, while the dove took its last peck at the window, and flew away. It was as if it had to wait, to hear my name called.

I entered the door of the Secretary's office with great anticipation. With words and a tone of kindness, she said to me that they had my 'transfer date,' to go to a 'Camp,' of my choice. Oh, my goodness! The joy I felt, rendered me speechless. The Secretary, asked for a response, "Did you hear me?" I had to snap out of my 'trance,' *"YES,"* I responded, although my heart was pumping in thankfulness, as *His* message was delivered to me by a 'Dove.'

The Tip:
"I put my hope in my Father; He inclined toward me and heeded my cry.
He lifted me out of the miry pit, the slimy clay and set my feet on a rock,
Steadied my legs; He put a new song into my mouth.
Many see and stand in awe and trust in the Most High.
Happy is the man that makes the Father his trust."
Psalm 40:1-5

CHAPTER 35

❖❖❖❖❖

No More Chains

Over thirty-five years ago, I said that I would never ride another Greyhound bus, after it took me almost a day and a half to get from New York City, visiting, back to Sumter, South Carolina. And when I couldn't bare being on the bus for another hour, as it made it to the South Carolina border, I called on one of my girlfriends, to come get me, pronto! And even though, the Greyhound bus, actually arrived to Sumter, SC before we did; that was just one hour longer, that I did not have to spend on it. A wasted trip? *No Siree*, not in my estimation. I was tired of being on that bus!

Here, it is, over thirty-five years, once again, and I am riding on a *'Greyhound'* bus! Which would be another day and a half. Perhaps, it was predestined for me to take these trips every thirty-five years on a Greyhound bus. If so, the next thirty-five years, I will be close to a hundred years old. Wonder where I'll be going to at that time in life? Just know, this time, however, I didn't mind taking this trip.

I was being furloughed, on this bus ride from a Federal Correctional Institution to a 'Camp,' in Florida. As we exited the Guard's station, the Town driver's vehicle was waiting to carry us to the bus terminal and I was overcome by being able to 'breathe.' It seemed like, 'different air,' and the fact that I didn't have to be escorted by an Officer, and further, no hands, waist, nor ankles in chains. "OH, WHAT A GOOD FEELING!" It felt good to open a car door, and put on a seat belt. All the little things we take for granted. I wanted to cry, but did not want the other women to see the tears, (though they were happy tears, this time). Nevertheless, I sucked it up and enjoyed the ride. I had prayed so hard for this day, and it was finally here.

When the bus arrived, to the designated terminal, I sat for a long moment, soaking in my surroundings. There would be a two-hour delay, on the departure from Dallas to Houston; so, I decided to walk with the other two women, to the store, which was visible from where we were stationed. The scenery was so beautiful; I was amazed. I was given a *whopping* forty-two dollars to buy food, but, at the moment, I didn't want any food; all I wanted was some '*watermelon*' flavored *Trident* chewing gum. (My favorite!). I couldn't believe that it had been several years, since I was even able to chew gum, and had to learn how to, it seemed… all over again, so I resorted to sucking it; since I kept biting the insides of my jaws. I wasn't about to throw my pack of gum away. Now, walking back from the store, I was captivated by everything around me; funny how that could happen; and I wasn't looking where I was going and almost got hit by a car. That would have been weird, 'furloughed inmate, get hit by a car.' But, I quickly jumped back onto the curb. Whew! A Lady laughed, and motioned to me, when to cross over. She probably knew that I was just leaving some sort of Institution, with my gray pants & shirt and my gray 'see-through' shoulder bag.

People were standing around talking, walking their dogs, waiting on the City Bus, and greeting strangers that walked past one another. It felt good smiling and saying, '*Hello*,' to the outside world. As the Gospel Artist, *Kirk Franklin's* song says, '*You look so much better when you smile*,' which I am a naturalist; when it comes to 'smiling.' And what made it so even that much more wonderful for me, was that I knew the Heavenly Host, was smiling with me, as I stood, in the midst, of the Creator's will.

My Sisters were so happy to know that I was traveling alone because, each time, in the past when they saw me, (in the Court room), I was always in chains, with an Escort nearby… that brought tears of sadness, to my eyes. At times, we were able to stop the tears from falling and at other times; we would just let them flow. Unrealistic expectations caused me a great deal of frustration. My only constant, was saying, "this too shall pass." I prayed many prayers, for this day, to be set free from the chains that held me captive. While, singing another favorite song by '*Mary*,

Mary,' of '*Take The Shackles Off My Feet.*' I've been set free from the chains that also held me bound, not only physically, but mentally as well. Those 'chains,' so to speak, tried so hard to keep me from becoming the Servant, that I had already been chosen 'to be.' No more iron rubbing as I walked, *HALLUEYAH*! Rubbing into my ankles, and I was able to hold a bottle of water. I know I serve an awesome Father… He may not come when it seems fitting to me, but I know that He is always on time.

As I got on the bus, I noticed that it was crowded. I had to push my way until I found a seat. I didn't care who was looking at me or what they were saying. I had to find a seat or wait another two hours for the next bus. I was determined that this bus was not going to leave me! My heart was beating uncontrollably, but once I found a seat and settled down, the Father sent '*peace,*' to rest upon me. And thus, the two and a half day journey had begun. It's so amazing to see the little things I took for granted; such as the beautiful sky, the green trees and flowers. The birds flying in unison. I was just so attentive to EVERYTHING. Also, everyone, around me had cellular phones. They were constantly on them, talking *and* texting. Technology had improved so much and had moved on so fast til I wondered what it felt like to actually talk on a phone. I wanted to ask the person sitting next to me, if I could use his cell phone, to call my Nephew, but was afraid that I would not know how to '*work it.*'

I was very reluctant to get off the bus at the first pit stop. There were too many, 'If's,' going through my mind; telling me, 'If,' you get off the bus, it might leave you… and you won't be able to run fast enough to catch it.' All I was thinking about, was 'what if,' I didn't make it to the 'Camp,' in the allotted time. Not realizing, at the moment, that I even had the 1-800 number for emergencies. Then, I used my better judgement, which I was getting more and more familiar with anyway, and got off the bus to get something to eat. The salad, was actually good, and so was, *believe it or not*, the bottle of spring water. Refreshing to my soul, in more ways than one. The sun soon began to set, and everyone on the bus had practically fell asleep, except, 'ME!' I was too excited… so I just stared out of the window and also read until I became sleepy. Then, shortly awakened by the Bus Driver's voice, alerting us where we were, and how long it would be before we'd arrive, and further mandated that everybody, '*had to,*' get off the bus for about two hours. After that, it was quite hard to go back to sleep for the duration of the ride, so I sang melodies, internally, meditated and watched the moon, and the bright stars, which were many. My experience led me to think of Abraham… when the Most High told him in Genesis, the 15th Chapter, verse 5, *"And He brought him forth abroad, and said, Look now toward heaven, and tell the stars if you be able to number them: and He said, so shall your seed be."*

The water flowing from the Gulf of Mexico, was breathtaking, when we arrived early the next morning, to Fort Walton, Florida. The awesomeness of our Creator, who causes the waters to flow from one end of the earth unto another, *'majestic.'* When the scripture in the 40th Chapter of Isaiah says, in verse 28 *'there is no searching of His understanding,'* don't even begin *to try* to figure Him out!

I began to think about the place that I was going to… I had heard many good things about it. For me, it was more freedom, and I was closer home. So exciting! The Bus Driver announced that within fifteen minutes, we would be at our *final destination.* Wow! It's time for me to step into the final stage before concluding this journey. All I could do, was to ask the Heavenly Father to keep me in the palm of His hands, and to protect me… that no evil would befall me and that I forever, while on His earth, continue to remain, free of chains!'

The Tip:
"And now behold, the chains
which were upon my hands are loose."
Jeremiah 40:4

CHAPTER 36

✦✦✦✦✦

My Praise Is A Weapon

"Oh, Father, how excellent is thy name, in all the Earth. Who has set they glory above the heavens. Out of the mouth of babes and sucklings has thou ordained strength, because of thine enemies, that thou mightiest be still the enemy and the avenger." (Psalms 8:1-2).

From the scripture, I see that the Father brought praise into existence. He ordained it, and put His stamp of approval on it. I see that it is a weapon that stop the enemy in its tracks and it is a weapon that I use to halt the enemy and his maneuvers.

As I continue to read on into the 9th Chapter of Psalm, beginning with verse 1; it says, *"I will praise thee, O' Father, with my whole heart; I will show forth thy marvelous works."* Verse 2, *"And I will be glad and rejoice in thee. I will sing praise to thy name, O' Most High,"* and Verse 3, *"when my enemies are turned back, they shall fall and perish at thy presence."*

I've come to understand that my praise is a weapon, and it is vital in my warfare against the force of the enemy. I will always offer up *sacrifice of praise* unto our Father; for it is He whose mercy is what endures forever. Look at Hebrews, Chapter 15, it speaks about how we '*must continue to offer the sacrifice of praise to our Father,*' not just sometimes or when we feel like it, but continually; and '*forget not that for with such sacrifice, the Father is well pleased.*' And the Most High, in 2nd Chronicles 5:13-14, reveals,

"As the trumpeters and singers were as one, to make one sound to be heard in praising and thanking the Father, and when they lifted up their voices with the trumpets and cymbals and instruments of music and praised the Most High, saying, He is good for His mercy endureth forever. That's when the house was filled with a cloud. The Priests couldn't stand to minister by reason of the cloud, for the glory of the Father had filled the House."

Just think about Israel, when they were crossing the Red Sea, how they were praising and thanking the Father for such a miracle and He was well pleased to use their praise as a weapon for Pharaoh and his Army. They didn't need a physical weapon of war! They only needed to sing praises to the Father.

When I praise the Father, and speak of His marvelous works, my faith rises within me and I begin experiencing the presence of Yahweh. The Scripture states that David praised the Father, so, til he danced out of his clothes, but notice what David said in Psalm 9:1-2, *"I will praise Thee... I will show forth all thy marvelous works. I will be glad and rejoice; I will sing praises."* I don't praise the Father because I feel like it; I praise Him because I want to praise Him. I praise Him because He is worthy of all the praise. Praise Him! Give Him the glory that is due unto His name! If you begin to praise Him, I will let you know for a surety, that He'll show up and show out, on your behalf. He will perform what He declares in His word.

I sing all the time, and can't hold not one note, just like one of my Sisters, but I know that the Father blesses us, for our will is to PRAISE HIM! It is good to know that our praises are a sweet smelling savor to our Father and that it is sincere and comes from the heart. Praise Him because you love Him. Praise Him, in spite of! Do you have, like myself, an *"In Spite of Praise?"* Well, if you do, or even if you don't, *"Praise Him, because there is none like Him! Praise him because when 'praises go up... blessings come down."*

I was being held in captivity, a Sister would always write me letters of encouragement. There was this one letter, that she wrote, that truly blessed me deeply. It was on 'Praising the Father," as I was going through my difficulty. She wrote, *"Praise the Father, in advance, and for what is taking place right now, for there is joy and peace in your praise and the most of all, your breakthrough is in your PRAISE."*

It is amazing how your praise can paralyze the enemy. It also defeats the enemy quicker than any physical battle plan. Isn't it great to know, that we were created to worship our Father, in the beauty of holiness?

The Tip:
"Let my soul live and it shall praise thee."

CHAPTER 37

❖❖❖❖❖

What's In Your 'Faith' Account?

Most of us have a bank account. It may consist of checking and a savings or an IRA. Some accounts you use to pay bills; while others you may use to enjoy plenty of material things; such as dining out or taking vacations; regardless to how you use your bank accounts; you make sure that the balance never goes into a negative balance as that would cause a decline in using the account and pay unnecessary charges. Thus, we try to make deposits as frequently as possible.

Once deposits are made, we have that assurance that when we get ready to use money from our various accounts, that the funds are actually available, so we can begin to reap the benefits! Well, let me discuss another account that is vital to our daily lives. It is our '*faith*' account. Which we all know, how to interpret this... yes, the same way, Hebrews 11:1, instructs us to... "*Now faith is the substance of things hoped for and the evidence of things not seen.*" You must be certain of what you hope for, first and foremost, and then certain of what you do not see! "*The just shall live by His faith.*" (Habakkuk 2:4).

Faith is the currency that you must use to transfer the Father's provision from the unseen realm of the spirit into the natural realm. Balance your faith account through daily prayers and supplications to keep from going into the negative. You should not have to encounter insufficient funds by using the bank of God; because His grace is SUFFICIENT enough! Take a few moments, to activate your account, by dropping the size of a grain of a mustard seed into it before using your it, as well, (Matthew 17:20). Small deposits go a long way. From the time you open your faith account, you must continue to build upon it!

Great spiritual rewards can be earned along the way, allowing you and I to make withdrawals from time to time. Currently, the bank will issue a 'debit card.' When I use my debit card, I become negligent and don't keep an accurate account of what I am spending, so I have to call to check my balance, and if it is too low, I immediately make a deposit, so I can continue to use my account. We must do the same thing when it comes down to our spiritual account. Run to the Father to refuel your faith account. This way you won't run into the red. Ask yourself sometime, "Do I have enough faith to produce victory on a daily basis? Or is my account running low, and no one can borrow anything from my life?"

Don't get me wrong, *'Emergencies,'* come up and you may have to make a huge faith withdrawal. In times like these, the Father, is a rewarder of them that diligently seeks him, and if you made those mustard seed deposits, along the way, you should have enough in your reservoir. There has to be a testimony of your faith to know that your ways have pleased the Father so you will be confident to withdraw a large amount from His fullness. This is what I call, "NOW FAITH!" Not faith to come, not the faith of tomorrow's faith, not next month's faith. Faith that I can use like we use the 'ATM,' 24/7.

I pray that when you make a withdrawal, that your faith is imputed for righteousness. I pray that our faith accounts are pleasing *to* the *Most High*, (Not Experian, TransUnion and Equifax). When I was faced, myself, with needing to make multiple calls to my Heavenly Father's bank of mercies; He granted my petitions and I know if He did it for me… He can do it for you too.

My fourth grandson was healed from having chronic seizures; my granddaughter's eye was miraculously healed. I, too, was healed from internal bleeding issues and spared from dying from the pangs of grief, all because I kept making faith deposits.

I've also learned that if you make a faith deposit and falter mid-stream; meaning that your faith is headed towards a negative balance (or turn in the storms of life as noted in the previous chapters), let me encourage you, to keep your faith account opened *still*. Don't try to swim in a pool without water. Also let the words of James, in Chapter 1:6, "*But let him ask in faith, nothing wavering. For he that wavereth is like a wave of the sea driven with the wind and tossed.*" Know that your faith will allow you to bend and not break.

If you have not opened a faith account, you need to do so 'quickly!' Regain your spiritual strength to be able to withdraw by faith to continue the good fight of FAITH!

The Tip:
"For we walk by faith and not by sight."
Hebrews 13:2

CHAPTER 38

Again, I Cried

Our ego can over power us when we lose sight of who we are; that's when you have to step back and regain your spiritual composure. Besides, being taken away from my family, so abruptly, didn't allow me a chance to tell them what happened; as there were plenty of lies and assumptions floating around. Which, was to be expected, when people don't know your circumstance. It happens all the time... *they will make up one for you.* Now that my family knows the truth; it didn't matter what anyone else thought. All I know is that, I love my family just as much as they love me. UNCONDITIONAL. The type of love that cannot be broken. *Much like how the Father loves us...* Even, in 1st Corinthians 13:4-6, we learn how to humbly love, if we only can adhere to it because *"Love suffers long and is kind, love does not envy; love does not parade itself; is not puffed up; does not behave rudely, does not seek its own; is not provoked; but rejoices in truth."*

By this particular time, in my life, I have experienced so many sleepless nights *and* years, then a time finally came... wherein it would be a *different day and a different cry...* Not like any other day that I might have cried. This day, I would get to embrace one of my Sisters; one of whom I haven't been able to physically touch, in a very long while, nor speak with. I saw her walk through the doors; she stood waiting; looking for me. When our eyes met; we began to smile. I was able to even reach out and touch her; that's when the floodgate of tears overtook the both of us. I now know how the character in the Movie, *The Colored Purple*, felt; after being separated from her Sister, for such a long time. We walked hand in hand, looking for a place to sit. Other people around us, may have thought we were unstable, but we didn't care what anyone else thought… As far as we were concerned, we were the only two in the room anyway and relied on, 1st Peter 4:8, *"And above all things have fervent love one for another; for 'love,' covers a multitude of sins."*

So happy to finally be in one another's company, *face to face*, all we could do is just stare at each other. Then, after we got over that initial shock, we began talking rapidly; jumping from one conversation to another; and I told her truthfully what happened in my situation, *before I was abruptly arrested* and taken from my family. *(I wasn't supposed to even be at my one Sister's house, but was led there… that leading, landing her and my Brother-in-Law, in jail that night. They felt my relatives was harboring a fugitive and all I was doing was visiting. They were released, thank goodness, but I had an 'Assignment').*

I was able to express how much it hurt not being able to attend our *Mother's* and *Sister's* funeral; and that's when I gazed into my Sister's eyes; and she looked just like Mama! AGAIN, I CRIED, cherishing the memory of our loved ones that passed on and all I had to do was keep reminding myself that my Father still had me *'in palm of his hands,'* (Isaiah 49:16).

My heart was beating so fast; as if it was about to pop out of my chest, as it was time for my Sister to leave 'me,' *this time*. We embraced and departed. I just wanted to make her my famous turkey-ham omelette, sip on a cup of tea, watch television with her and finish our lengthy conversations. Again, I cried because I just wanted to hear her sing her favorite song by *Whitney Houston, "I Wanna Dance With Somebody."* But until the next appointed time, I will wait with expectancy, knowing that the Father hears us and our time on this *'different day,'* was of great value. You cannot place value on love… its priceless!

The Tip:
"The righteous cry out; and the Father hears them."
Psalms 34:7

CHAPTER 39

✦✦✦✦

A Covenant of Protection

While being held in captivity, there were many arrows thrust out to wound me, mentally, emotionally and physically. I began to ask *and* believe by faith, that my Heavenly Father would pick me up out of a *miry clay*, and deliver me from my calamity. There had been so much that He had ALREADY rescued me from and looking at it in the natural sense, it seemed pretty dismal. Yet I had something that the enemy did not possess… I had a *"Covenant of Protection!"*

A *'Covenant of Protection,'* plainly signifies that my Heavenly Father is faithful to keep His promises and guard us from any evil that may *try* to befall us. And the things *that seemed to* be impossible for me to overcome; *was not* impossible with Him, as the Book of Luke, Chapter 1 and verse 37, so graciously reminds us of, *"For with the Father; nothing shall be impossible!"*

Likewise, Deuteronomy 28:7, was not written as an afterthought, it was written for our purpose; to know that the enemy has no jurisdiction over us. *"Yahweh shall cause your enemies that rise up against you to be smitten before your face; they shall come out against you one way, and flee before you seven ways,"* and verse 10 continues that same *protection. "And all the people of the earth shall see that 'you are called' by the name of Yahweh, and they shall be afraid OF YOU!* So, the enemy can try to use all the scare tactics he wants to; but they will falter, for the Most High, *"has given meat unto them that fear Him; He will ever be mindful of His covenant,"* (Psalm 111:5).

The enemy expected me to fold and give up; especially under the intense pressure of betrayal, (knowing that there were people using someone very close and dear, *to me*, to help them build a bogus case). That was quite disheartening, to say the least; but I refused to buckle under the weight and I refused to be afraid. I had been called, by *the Most High*, for a purpose; way before the enemy sought to destroy me, *rather I believed it or not*. And yes, at times, when I myself, would even frustrate my own purpose; it still did not take away the Heavenly Father's purpose *for my life*. He knew me while I was yet in my Mother's womb, as pronounced in Psalm 139:13, *"For thou hast possessed my reins; thou hast 'covered me' in my Mother's womb."* I was birthed with this *'Covenant of Protection'* which was in place all along. I was not going to be defeated by the enemy and neither shall you!

The Tip:
"The Father leads with unfailing love and faithfulness,
all those who keep His Covenant and obey His decrees."
Psalms 25:10

C H A P T E R   4 0

◆◆◆◆◆◆

Healing Allowed

I was at work, September 15, 2015, thinking about the '*next day*,' which would be the Anniversary date of my Husband's death. The past eight years, '*a whirlwind*.' *Wow*! Time just kept moving right on, while I was trying to stand still. I began to reminisce... all that were left... *were memories*... I tried to steady my breathing but suddenly a sharp pain pierced inside of my chest. A couple of months earlier, I had been experiencing shortness of breath just while talking; which was very uncomfortable. But this one morning, my breath didn't wait on me to speak. As I reached to wipe a window in the Unit's television room, I hit the floor, "*BANG!*"

There I was, laid out, unconscious, on the cement floor. As I came too, I tried to get up, but couldn't and that's when the Most High dispatched one of *His Angels*, a wonderful woman, to come help me until medical staff arrived. Once the medical team showed up; they were trying very hard to keep me calm, as they administered oxygen, right away; then placed me on a stretcher, to wheel me down to the Nurses Station. The Nurses took my vitals, and gave me some medicine; while another called for an ambulance, so I could be transported to the nearest hospital.

I was in a state of unbelief... this can't be happening to me! Now, fear really came upon me, as if it was *Pentecost*, in the form of a rushing mighty wind... '*NOT AGAIN!*' I began to pray, saying to myself, "*I am not afraid*." I knew I was having a heart attack! But cardiac arrest, was not going to rule today! I'd come too far, with the grace and mercy of my Heavenly Father, and I did not... and would not... believe that HE would bring me this far to leave me. "*But I see another law,*" Romans, Chapter 7, verse 23 says, "*in my members, warring against the law of my mind, and bringing me into captivity…*" NO! I '*was*' going home within several months; *THIS CAN'T BE HAPPENING*! It was like a scene from a movie; being played out. I couldn't cry because I was trying to preserve my breathing and besides by now, I'm sure my tear ducts, had all but took wings and flew away! My breathing continued, *by the second*, to become shorter and shorter.

Counselors yelled that the ambulance was taking far too long; and that's when I perceived something was terribly wrong; since you were '*just another number,*' if you died, you just died, in this setting. But to hear clamoring concern for my *wellbeing*, took this scenario to a whole different level. It didn't help that I began to envision all the faces of my love ones, *my two sons, my grandchildren, daughter-in-laws, my siblings, my family…* "*FATHER, I NEED YOUR HELP!*" My mind reverberated back to what it knew best… I recalled, stored up scriptures, from '*The Menu,*' (the Word), itself… "*Yea, though I walk through the valley of the shadow of death, I will fear no evil, for thou art with me…*" (Psalms 23:4).

I felt a presence nearby, something unseen, but close. Peace surrounded me, like a comforting blanket. I felt safe from whatever sickness that was lurking. "*But the comforter,*" John 14:26-27 declares, "*which is the Holy Spirit, whom the Father will send in My name, He shall teach you all things, and bring all things to your remembrance, whatsoever, I have said unto you. Peace, I leave with you, My peace, I give unto you; not as the world gives; give I unto you; let not your heart be troubled, neither let it be afraid.*"

As I was admitted to the hospital, there of course, were certain restrictions… "*No visiting,* FROM ANYONE, *rather inside, nor family on the outside…* no telephone use, first call, last call, NO CALLS… I was still in the custody of the Bureau of Prisons ("BOP"). Yet, there was already an '*UNSEEN VISITOR,*' who was *already* on the scene. *HALLEUYAH*!

The Nurses made sure that I was comfortable with everything that I needed *and* wanted. (*Don't you just love resting your feet upon your 'FOOTSTOOL'*). Now, I was completely worn out, from all of the medication, and drifted off into a deep sleep; only to be disturbed by the Nurses, to take my vitals, prep me for a series of test, and change the IV bag. Further tests would be warranted, as the results of some of the tests came back inconclusive.

It's the wee-hours of the morning; I am perplexed on every side, as I contemplate the heart procedure that had to take place within several hours.

Again, I regurgitate, some much needed *'Appetizers,'* (*Prayers*) and begin to talk to my Heavenly Father... *"Yahweh, nothing gives me more comfort, but to know that every time I pray, you hear me. I may not be able to see you, but I know that you are near and that you have given your Angels charge over me,"* (Psalm 91:11). *"You promised that through obedience, you will take away sickness,* (Exodus 23:25), *so being a Servant of yours, I am asking you to heal me; because a weak heart will not serve your purpose in order for me to continue on this journey, on Earth. There is nothing more reliable than your promises, and right now, I am refusing to waver. I am solely trusting and believing in your word, that all is going to be well concerning this procedure. In Yahshua's name, Amen!"*

I am now in the Operating Room, and the Doctor is preparing to administer the medication within the IV tube, *to put me to sleep.* The Nurse told me that I would go to la-la land in about a minute or so... and as Operating Room humor would have it; they all said, *"Goodnight!"* But I couldn't go to sleep, because there was a light in the corner of the room that no one was able to see, *but me.* From that focal point, a reassuring voice touched my mind, *"Don't be afraid, for I am with you, I will never leave you, nor forsake you."* And there again, was that peace, that covered. Sleep never fell upon me; therefore, I watched the Doctor as he performed the procedure.

Hours later, the Doctor came with the test results... There were no blockages within the arteries to my heart... *"WOW,"* was all I could muster, and a sigh of... *"THANK YOU FATHER!"*

Upon my release, the Nurse Supervisor paid me a visit. She asked of my stay and how I was treated while in their care. *"Everyone treated me well, and with respect,"* I responded. She then smiled, and reported, 'all of her Nurses lamented that I was *'one quiet patient... who did not complain about anything.'* I wanted to, *so tell her,* that it was because my *'Unseen Visitor,'* made sure that I was okay.

Present day, *I'm FREE!* And although, I still have some bouts with shortness of breath; it is a sure sign, that I am talking *too much or too fast*; and that's when I slow it down, regroup, relish in the deliverance that my Heavenly Father granted unto me and whisper... *HEALING ALLOWED! And it is so!*

The Tip:
"O' Father, My Creator, I cried unto thee
and thou hast healed me."
Psalms 30:2

"TO MY PATRONS"

OH, MAY, "THE MENU,"
HAVE SERVED YOU WHAT WAS NEEDED
TO SUSTAIN YOUR WELL-BEING!

I PRAY YOU RICHLY ENJOYED
INDULGING IN THE
MANY APPETIZERS
AND THE
FULL COURSE MEALS
(THE ENTIRE CHAPTER)

I PRAY YOU GAINED PLENTY
OF SPIRITUAL INSIGHT
FROM DINING!

ORDER FROM THE MENU,
ANY DAY OR EVERY DAY
AT NO
EXTRA CHARGE!

UNTIL YOU RETURN.... I LEAVE YOU WITH
THE ONLY DESSERT ON
"THE MENU"
A YUMMY SCOOP
OF
"GRATEFULNESS"

J. Globadiyah

Printed in the United States
By Bookmasters